THE BIG APPLE CHRONICLES
NEW YORK

TRAVEL TALES AND TIPS

WADDLE THE WORLD WITH RED PENGUIN BOOKS

THE BIG APPLE CHRONICLES

NEW YORK

Featuring:
Steve Borodkin – Katrenia Busch – Paul DiSclafani
Richard Harries – Dennis Hawkins – Mark Fleisher
Jordan M. Frazier – Suzanne Kamata – Michael P. Kusen
Mark Lord – Antoinette Truglio Martin
Lisa Diaz Meyer – William John Rostron
Laura Shenton – Hanna Swanepoel – Jim Tritten
Janet Metz Walter – Lynn Zimmering

**WADDLE THE WORLD WITH
RED PENGUIN BOOKS**

New York: The Big Apple Chronicles

Copyright © 2025

All rights reserved.

Published by Red Penguin Books

Bellerose Village, NY

ISBN

Digital 978-1-63777-741-1

Print 978-1-63777-742-8

No part of this book may be reproduced in any form or by any electronic or mechanical means, including information storage and retrieval systems, without written permission from the author, except for the use of brief quotations in a book review.

contents

A FISH STORY By Antoinette Truglio Martin (from "Becoming America's Food Stories")	1
MEATBALLS ON A FORK By Antoinette Truglio Martin (from "Becoming America's Food Stories")	7
THE TWO CARROT RING AND THE CENTRAL PARK CHARM By Janet Metz Walter (from "The 2 Carrot Ring")	11
LET'S TAKE A WALK *The differences between then and now.* By Lynn Zimmering (from "My Pandemic Paradox")	17
ADJUSTING TO CITY LIFE AS AN OLDSTER *Here's how my ninety-year-old body and mind have coped* By Lynn Zimmering (from "My Pandemic Paradox")	21
ETHEL MERMAN AND OTHER CELEBRITY ENCOUNTERS By Mark Lord (from "The Theater and I")	27
THE ANGEL FROM BROOKLYN By Paul DiSclafani (from "Long Island Living")	33
THE NIGHT THE LIGHTS WENT OUT IN BROOKLYN By Paul DiSclafani (from "Long Island Living")	37
3 DAYS IN OCTOBER by Mark Fleisher	41
A STAY AT THE ALGONQUIN HOTEL By Suzanne Kamata	45
OLD NEIGHBORHOOD (1970'S) By Lisa Diaz Meyer	49
A WEEKEND IN NEW YORK by Richard Harries	51

MY SECOND TRIP TO BLOOD BROTHERS
(PETULA AND BROADWAY)   55
By Richard Harries

TAKE ME BACK TO BROOKLYN, PLEASE   59
by Mark Fleisher

I AM FROM ...   63
by Jim Tritten

THIS TOWN   67
by Jordan M Frazier

THAT AWAKENS WITH THE SLEEPLESS
CITY   69
by Katrenia Busch

THE LITTLE BOOK THAT DID   71
by Mark Fleisher

FATED MEETING IN NYC   75
By Janet Metz Walter

HEADLINES   89
By Dennis Hawkins

GRANDPA ABE   93
By Steve Borodkin

THE KING AND THE LOWER EAST SIDE   99
By Steve Borodkin

THE RATS OF NEW YORK CITY   103
by Laura Shenton

THE BOBBLEHEAD   107
by William John Rostron

IN THE HEIGHTS: ANOTHER SIDE OF NEW
YORK CITY   115
by William John Rostron

THE BIG WALK   127
Michael P. Kusen

About the Authors   139
Also From Travel Tales & Tips   147

a fish story

By Antoinette Truglio Martin (from "Becoming America's Food Stories")

There is a treasure trove of fish stories around my family's table. Fishing has and still is a great family pastime that is shared among the generations of men, women and children.

The love of the sea and the need to hold a fishing pole probably stemmed from the family's Sicilian and southern Italian roots. If they didn't farm or cut stone, they fished. The original homes most of the ancestors came from were in fishing villages. They weaved nets, set lines, and launched dories each morning and returned at the end of the day with the bounty.

My dad and uncles kept boats in varying degrees of repair and seaworthiness just so we could all get to a beach or go fishing. As small children, my siblings, cousins, and I were given some form of a fishing pole to pull in our catch. Snappers and blowfish were in abundance back then. We all got caught up in the excitement and awe of the fascinating creatures, especially the blowfish that blew up onto a prickly ball and made croaking sounds.

Fish dishes were always on the family weekly menu. We Catholics marked Fridays as fish day—no meat, but during the summer, fish meals showed up more frequently. Grandma Truglio, who would not eat the incredible fish and seafood dishes she cooked, made trays of baked blowfish tails, snappers, and bluefish we had caught. The summer table talk swelled with fish tales.

The Sunfish story has a few versions but Aunt Marsha told the best one. One summer afternoon my dad and uncles putt-putt home from a day of fishing off the Fire Island inlet. They had strapped a two- hundred-pound sunfish to the side of the 25' Higgins.

A sunfish is a peculiar fish. Their huge bodies look like a giant flat head with a short tail. The fins are seemingly too small and narrow to enable a graceful swim or quick get away from predators. Sunfish can be spotted on the ocean surface, carelessly flopping their pectoral fins while slurping jellyfish.

My dad and uncles had never seen a sunfish before and thought the catch would provide days of meals. At the time, the sunfish was the biggest fish they had ever caught and there was nothing better than actual proof of their incredible fish story. They pulled into the canal behind Uncle Tom's house and hauled the sunfish onto the lawn. A rag-tag parade of aunts, grandmas, and little kids marched down the street from the Country House to see the prize. Everyone marveled.

Everyone, except Great Grandma. She took one look at the sunfish and shook her head.

"Dig a hole. Bury it!" she commanded in Sicilian.

"But Grandma, it is such a big fish. Something could be eaten."

"No. Bury it."

"Is it poisonous?" asked Uncle Tom.

"No. Bury it in a deep hole so it doesn't infect the garden." said Great Grandma. She stomped off back to the Country House.

"If it's not poisonous," reasoned Uncle Tom to his daughter-in-law, Marsha, "something could be eaten."

As it turned out, the sunfish yielded a very small amount of flesh. The meat was white and looked clean, but Uncle Tom boiled a piece, just in case it was poisonous. Uncle Tom and Aunt Marsha handed out a taste for all of the onlookers. Within seconds burning pin and needle sensations invaded their tongues and lips. The pain could not be washed away with water or beer. The whole sunfish was buried in an extra deep hole, away from the garden and grape arbor.

I imagine Great Grandma had known sunfish. She grew up in Castellammarre del Golfo, a fishing village along the Sicilian coast. Since sunfish eat only jellyfish, their small amount of meat is inedible, and, according to Great Grandma, not even worth fertilizing the garden.

Blowfish were an easy catch and abundant in the Great South Bay on the south shore of Long Island. They were everywhere—along the piers, in the seaweed grassland, and in a million secret fishing holes.

Dad would fasten a small hook at the end of a string for each little kid in our tremendous brood. He taught us to bait a hook with a shiner we caught in seining nets earlier in the day. We threw our lines over the dock or boat railing. The first big lesson was to remember to hold onto the other end of the string. In no time, (it must have been within seconds because I do not remember any of my siblings or cousins with an attention span that lasted more than a minute), a tiny shake, a tug, and finally a pull brought up a buck-tooth blowfish.

Bluefishing was exciting and required a boat ride to the inlet, heavier poles, reliable reels and sharp hooks. Striped bass, however, was the prize of a fishing expedition. These beautiful fish offered a delicate white meat that did not require a good deal of fuss to prepare.

Nonna called striped bass spindella, because of its strong dorsal fin. She opened the whole fish flat on a baking dish, sprinkled her bread crumbs on top and a generous drizzle of olive oil. She folded the fish back together and popped it into a 350° oven. Dad said that Nonna liked to keep the head on, but Grandma Truglio insisted the heads be buried with the guts, since she did not like to look at the eyes.

Bluefish, a gamier meat, needed additional attention. Grandma Truglio shook salt and pepper on top, added bread crumbs and onion slices then wrapped it in foil to bake in a 350° oven or on a charcoal grill.

Blowfish tasted better than any chicken nugget (they were not yet invented when I was a kid). Grandma Truglio sprinkled salt, pepper, and bread crumbs on the blowfish tails, generously drizzled olive oil on top, and baked them in a 350° oven until brown. They were quickly devoured with a side of ketchup.

meatballs on a fork

By Antoinette Truglio Martin (from "Becoming America's Food Stories")

Sundays were macaroni and meatball days. Mom would start the sauce first thing in the morning. She claimed that my little brother, Billy Boy, wouldn't know the next day was Monday if he didn't have macaroni and meatballs on Sunday.

When I was a kid, Sundays were spent in Brooklyn at Grandma Truglio's. The staircase and second floor flat were filled with the aromas of garlic, tomatoes, the trinity (oregano, basil, and parsley), and a roast. Grandma chopped, pinched, stirred, rolled meatballs, and checked the oven throughout the morning. Company was coming for a day of celebrating anything and eating. An endless parade of dishes filled with macaroni, assorted vegetables, and meats adorned the dining room table.

My mom took on this role when Grandma moved from Brooklyn to Long Island. The sauce was put up first thing in the morning. I would wake up to the wafts of garlic and onion. Mom made the meatballs, cleaned whatever vegetable she had planned as a side dish, and dressed the roast. Company was coming. Mom was determined to feed the masses. If there were no leftovers, then someone surely went home hungry.

Once the meatballs were mixed, rolled, then baked, they simmered in the sauce. You could smell the inviting warmth all day. Heaven.

Lunchtime never happened on Sundays. Dinner started at

about 2:00 in the afternoon. If someone got hungry before company arrived, before the cheese, olives, and crackers came out, they had to ask Mom what there was to eat. The last thing Mom wanted to do was to stop the prepping and make a cranky kid or hungry husband a sandwich. Instead, Mom took a fork and stabbed a meatball simmering in the pot of sauce. She placed a paper towel under the dripping prize.

"Eat this. Don't make a mess!" she instructed. A meatball on a fork was the best pre-appetizer.

Through the years, Mom's grandchildren came to know the Sunday dinner routine. Mom's most cherished compliment was when her grandson, Michael, walked into her house and announced, "It smells like Sunday at Grandma's!" His reward was a kiss and a meatball on a fork. To this day, the routine still occurs.

Meatball recipes evolved over the years. Most of my sisters use chopped beef, seasoned bread crumbs, milk, or water. My cousin, Lorraine, adds raisins as her Sicilian grandmother had done. Some roll huge meatballs, like a mini meatloaf, while others fashion baby-size spheres. It is a personal preference dictated by what the cook's family craves.

SUNDAY MEATBALLS

1 to 1½-pound of chopped beef and pork. If there was a sale, I would splurge on the beef, pork, and veal package.

finely chopped ½ onion and 2 cloves of garlic (roasted garlic is best)

olive oil

seasoned bread crumbs

grated parmesan or romano cheese

1 egg

pesto

salt and pepper to taste

oregano and parsley (if fresh, chop very fine or use a mini food processor to pulverize with a bit of oil)

Sauté chopped onion and roasted garlic in a splash of olive oil until the onions are translucent. Let it cool.

Add the egg to the meat, mix. Add the sautéed onions, garlic, the oregano, parsley, salt, and pepper. Incorporate equal amounts of bread crumbs and cheese, and handmix everything until you reach the desired texture.

Take a palm-size portion of the meat mixture, roll into a ball, and place on a cookie tray.

Bake the meatballs in a 350°F oven for about 20-30 minutes. Let cool in a bowl with paper towels to absorb excess fat. Place the meatballs into a pot of sauce.

Fend off anyone claiming to be a taste tester unless they earned a meatball on a fork.

the two carrot ring and the central park charm

By Janet Metz Walter (from "The 2 Carrot Ring")

When my father George and his twin brother came home from the service after WWII, they moved back in with their widowed father. He gave them both jobs in his advertising and display business.

My father was actually very artistic and talented, and he learned the business well. As the business expanded, they found a need for a bookkeeper; and they hired a lady named Phyllis who applied for the job.

My father was very personable with a great sense of humor, and he flirted with all the women in the company. Employees were forbidden to date each other, but my grandfather thought that Phyllis might be nice for my father's brother who was much quieter and more subdued than my father, so they went out on a couple of dates. But Phyllis was more interested in George, the brother who always made her laugh.

When she told her mother how charming and funny George was, her mother was not happy. "You need this job," she told her daughter. "You cannot risk getting fired by dating the boss's son when it is forbidden."

But Phyllis really liked the boss's son; and he was really getting to like her, too. They were very comfortable together and developed a very nice relationship. So Phyllis had to be very careful about how she interacted with George at work; but they found ways to be together, both during working hours and after work.

They said they weren't really dates because he never spent money on her. His father didn't pay him a very good salary even though he was a very good worker; but since he was living at home and not paying room and board, his father did not see the need to pay him a lot of money. But George was very resourceful. He found lots of free places to take Phyllis.

They would go to free museums and browse the exhibits at the art museums, paintings, and sculptures by famous artists. At The Museum of Natural History, there were dinosaurs whose bones stretched from one end of a room to the other and fascinating colorful exhibits of natural gemstones and ones that were set into the jewelry of royalty.

They would walk up and down Fifth Avenue at Christmas time to see the lights and look at the decorated windows in the big department stores.

The nicest time, however, was lunchtime. The office was close to Central Park and their favorite thing to do on a nice day was to sit on a bench in the park and share a sandwich. They would talk or watch birds or people watch. They had a favorite bench in the park that they would always sit on. It always seemed to be waiting for them.

As time passed George realized that he was in love with Phyllis as she was with him. He was ready to propose.

Diamonds are measured in carat weight. For jewelry, they are cut into sizes from tiny stones that could weigh 1/10 of a carat to huge stones that could weigh ten carats or more. Most engagement rings at the time averaged anywhere from ¼ of a carat to 2 carats. But George couldn't really afford a nice ring.

At the time Woolworth's sold silly "two carrot" rings that were actually two little plastic carrots. So after 10 months, George bought Phyllis a two carrot ring from Woolworth's and proposed.

. . .

They were married in 1949. My father went on to start his own advertising and display business and they started a family.

About five years later, he was doing well and decided to design a gift for my mother. He had a lot of friends in the jewelry industry on 47th Street. He designed a gold charm that depicted their bench in Central Park with the lamp post, the birds and even the street sign. He took the drawing to one of his jeweler friends who made up the charm for him.

The charm had a big circle of gold around it but it was too big for my mother to wear around her neck so she had the large gold circle removed. A few years later my father designed a bracelet for her to hang the charm from. Charm bracelets were very popular at that time.

Eventually, they moved to Long Island to raise their family. They enjoyed a happy life. There would be other presents of jewelry but nothing as special as that charm.

On my mother and father's 50th wedding anniversary in 1999, my father arranged for them to stay in the Plaza Hotel near Central Park and to go into the park in the afternoon and sit on their bench which had been changed, but it was fine. It was a beautiful Anniversary. They were always perfect for each other.

By the way, the back of the charm is inscribed "This is our life, 7/48 till forever." That's when they first dated, July 1948.

THIS IS WHERE
This is where I fell in love,
With a summer moon high up above.
But oh that was so long ago,
Sixty plus years or so.
As we sat in Central Park,
The sun went down, it was almost dark.
He stole a kiss, just one that night.
That was the start of a love so right.

Life is not simple, there's always a wrinkle.
He was my boss's son, this boy with a twinkle.
I'd be fired for sure, if his father should know,
And the job came first, before any beau.
But he broke down my defenses with one more kiss,
And then another, I couldn't resist.
He hadn't a job, he didn't have any money,
So we'd meet at the bench, whether rainy or sunny.
That was so very long ago,
And we were so in love.
We married a few months later,
With blessings from above.
The years went by, they truly flew.
Soon it was fifty and we knew what we'd do.
We went to sit in the park once more,
Just as we had done before.
They changed the bench,
The one we claimed, but it didn't matter now.
It was there when we first fell in love,
And "this is where" somehow.

let's take a walk

The differences between then and now.

By Lynn Zimmering (from "My Pandemic Paradox")

Growing up in upper Manhattan, walking was a natural part of my everyday existence, except we were a family with a car. During the war years 1940 to 1945, we gave up having one. With rationing and the war effort, gasoline was scarce, mechanics were mostly fighting as soldiers, and it was unpatriotic to divert attention from the war effort to a private family.

Right after the war ended, my father bought a new car. It was a complete redesign of a Buick with long, sleek fenders in baby blue. It was so beautiful that it was stolen about two weeks after he bought it.

We lived on Fort Washington Avenue, just north of 187th Street. The nearest subway entrance was up a long, steep hill on 183rd. I only noticed it was a hill once I started wearing high heels. How shapely our legs looked was more important than how our feet felt as teenagers. High heels gave us pain but also confidence.

My apartment building was across the Street from my elementary school—indeed, no problem getting there. However, once I got to High School, I needed to use public transportation as my school was on 135th Street and Convent Avenue.

I frequently walked up the hill to the subway entrance carrying my purse, my books, and my French horn in its bulky case (I played the French horn in high school.) Or I would take the bus from my nearby corner, which left me at 135th Street and Broadway, to be followed by a schlep with all my stuff up the hill to Convent Avenue. But the hills were of little importance to me. I was young and strong.

After college, my first job was as a member of the Executive Training Squad at Bloomingdales on 59th Street. Once again, it meant a daily trek up the hill to the subway, which left me at 59th Street but on the Westside. Sometimes, I would walk across town. If you've ever worked in a department store, I'm sure you remember that the job required being on your feet all day. I can hardly believe my stamina, walking to the subway, across town from Eighth Avenue to Lexington, and working on my feet all day.

I got around mostly in my car from those years until now. Whether in Providence, R.I. or Hackensack, N.J., it was a car. For years and years, I hardly walked at all. When I came from Hackensack to the city for an event like a doctor's appointment or a haircut, I would park my car in the least expensive lot I could find and then walk to my destination. These garages were either on Twelfth or First Avenues, but —it didn't matter. I never considered the walk to be difficult.

Then came the pandemic, and like everyone else, I stayed home. My body aged faster because of the forced inactivity. Fast forward to me today. My ninetieth birthday is coming up in May, and I live in the city and have no car. This is challenging. As an NYC resident, I need to find flat or downhill streets to walk on. Hills have become my archenemy. They leave me breathless and make my legs ache. I hope the more I walk, the stronger I will become.

Every day, I plan a little walking expedition. I keep track of my steps on my Apple watch. I'm not a fan of walking randomly. But, with a specific destination, I can walk a mile. Not too bad for such an old person!

Remember, aging only matters if you are a cheese.

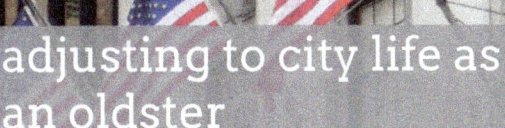

adjusting to city life as an oldster

Here's how my ninety-year-old body and mind have coped

By Lynn Zimmering (from "My Pandemic Paradox")

When I moved to New York City last September, what I had envisioned was different from how it turned out. I pictured myself attending museums, concerts, and dance recitals daily. I imagined frequently eating luxurious foods in exotic restaurants. Since I had given up my car, I knew the city offered convenient public transportation to take me where I needed to go. So, I anticipated living the "Good Life."

Before I give you the wrong impression, I want to be clear about my current situation. I **love** living in the city but had to adapt to find contentment and pleasure. For example, it took me six months to finally get to the Metropolitan Museum, within walking distance of my apartment.

Here's what I did.

#1, First and foremost, acceptance of being old is a significant undertaking wherever I live. It's the critical element.

Time changes you as you age. When I was younger, I packed as much activity into my days as possible. If I noticed an extra half hour somewhere, I would stick an activity into that space for my time management efficiency.

Now, acknowledging my age, I have less to do. Rather than moping around, I relish my peaceful times. Sometimes, I read or write blogs, nap, or sit on my terrace to watch the construction across the street. It's all OK.

#2, Giving up my car prevents me from visiting my N.J. friends. I miss them, although they come to see me. I know very few people who live in the city to hang out with, but since my daughter and her family live in my building, I'm grateful for their attentiveness. Also, it's easier for my sons to visit me since I'm closer to their homes.

#3, I expected to use the subway, the transportation that supplies the most convenient and speedy way to travel, but it was deemed unsuitable or safe for me by my family. They are correct, as I'm a bit unsteady on my feet, and an accidental push might knock me to the ground with a broken something.

#4, The buses are another option and expedient. They can accommodate people of all ages. They are accessible to shopping carts, baby carriages, and wheelchairs and even dip down to the street level for easy boarding. They run often, and the bus drivers are kind and helpful. The hardest part of the bus system is finding the bus stops for my trips back home. My senior bus and subway pass allows me to travel from one end of the city to another for a little more than a dollar. It's the cheapest way around.

#5 While on the subject, I didn't realize how expensive everything is in the city. All my financial planning went out the window as the bills started rolling in. Amazon is my savior, with low prices and free delivery. You can't beat it.

My apartment feels like it's in the middle of a shopping mall. I can walk to Fairway, The Gap, Old Navy, Target, H&M, Lululemon, the Post Office, the bank, and other shops, including Shake Shack. Being exposed to the activity level in my neighborhood is fun. There are people of all sizes, ethnicities, and ages. Everybody fits in. I deal with the high prices as best I can.

#6, Getting anywhere by bus takes a significant amount of time. I finally realized that it didn't matter to me how long it takes to complete my journey because I have all the time in the world, so who cares? My favorite walk is along Fifth Avenue, on the park side, because there are benches along the way; it's shady and level. I can stop and rest when I need to do so. I arrive too early or late due to my lack of experience with buses and traffic. But I'm learning how long I need for each trip.

#7, Besides buses, I was expecting to walk to wherever I needed to go. New York is a walking city. The only problem is I have developed an annoying shortness of breath and lost my stamina. Maybe it's because of staying home for two years as protection from COVID-19, or perhaps because I am two years older.

#8, My local streets have many hills, and while I'm OK with walking down hills, I have a problem with walking uphill due to my breathing. That means I have become an expert at finding downhill streets, but my return trips are challenging. It's inevitable. I walk up hills to get home. It's all part of my adjustment to city life.

#9, Keeping up with my doctor's visits is essential for my health. I regularly see an endocrinologist, cardiologist, urologist, ophthalmologist, pulmonologist, dermatologist, neurologist, and podiatrist. Can you believe it? No wonder it takes up so much time.

What I've been doing is combining long walks and doctor's visits. These become all-day activities as I walk pretty slowly.

I live about halfway between Mt. Sinai at 100th St. and Fifth Ave. and Weill Cornell hospitals and their doctors at 70th St. and York. My goal is to walk between three thousand and ten thousand steps daily. I prefer a destination to pointless wandering, so doctor's visits fill the bill.

#10, Something is always going on or up in the city. Since I've been here, a new high-rise dwelling has been going up across the street, creating lots of noise and dirt. It has also blocked my view. However, it's exciting watching its development. That's the city, you know.

So, these are my issues. I am amazingly comfortable in my new apartment even though I end up with less space every time I move. I'm getting used to not having as much to do as I did in my prior years. As I take rests during the day, on my sofa or terrace. I remind myself that resting isn't "nothing to do." It has become my newest activity.

ethel merman and other celebrity encounters

By Mark Lord (from "The Theater and I")

In case you couldn't guess, I am star struck.

I've waited at many a stage door at the conclusion of a performance, hoping to catch a glimpse of the performers.

Heck, I've waited at many a stage door even when I hadn't just seen the show. In passing, I'd see a bunch of people gathered in front of one of the Broadway theaters and race over to find out who everyone was waiting for. Most of the time, I'd dart into the theater, pick up a Playbill, and join the crowd.

In those days, a much more innocent time and long before security was so tight, it was relatively easy to enter a theater, as well as most everywhere. How else could so many of us have "second-acted" so many shows without ever getting into trouble?

Those like us who hung around theaters used to be known— way before my time—as "stage door Johnnies," a term going back to the early 1900s. Back then it specifically referred to men who spent a lot of time at a theater in the hopes of gaining the romantic attention of an actress.

Our intentions were less lofty. If we were lucky, we'd come away with a photo or two with our favorite celebrities and, perhaps, some new autographs to add to our collections.

This calls to mind a man who was known all around the Broadway theater district in the 1970s. He appeared to be middle-aged, was always disheveled, and walked around with stacks of autographs, mostly on index cards, that he had amassed over the years.

He would walk up to someone—innocent people just walking up or down the street included—and ask if he or she was in show business. He didn't care who they were or how famous they might have been. If they were even remotely connected to the theater, he wanted their autographs.

He seemed to be everywhere, all the time. Autograph hunting appeared to be his full-time occupation. I overheard many a conversation between him and a star as he approached for an autograph. "Oh, come on, you must have me about six times already," they would say, or something close to that. It didn't matter. He would insist on yet another and they usually obliged. And, mind you, those were the days before people made a living selling this sort of thing on eBay!

But I digress—again! I've had many memorable experiences "stage dooring," and not just at Broadway shows. I spent more than a few summer afternoons during my high school and college years attending tapings of the television shows that were based in New York.

The David Frost Show, a syndicated talk series that ran from 1969 to 1972, was taped at what was then known as The Little Theatre, the name still visible on the building's 44th Street facade. It was later to be renamed for the first lady of the American theater, **Helen Hayes**, after the original theater bearing her name, two blocks away on 46th Street, was torn down in 1982, along with the Morosco and the Bijou, to make way for a new hotel, the New York Marriott Marquis.

I spent most of my vacation from school attending tapings of the show, which featured many well-known stars of the day, including **Julie Andrews**.

She happened to be the guest on Frost's birthday and in a pre-planned surprise for him, the audience joined Miss Andrews in singing "Happy Birthday" to him. I still refer to this as the time I sang with **Julie Andrews** on national television!

Unfortunately, I was unable to get Miss Andrews' autograph

on that occasion, but I did meet up with her years later—the date was October 11, 1999—at the Barnes & Noble bookstore on Broadway at 66th Street for a book signing for her then-new children's publication, *Little Bo, The Story of Bonnie Boadicea*. Inside the front cover she signed her name as "**Julie Andrews Edwards**," her last name taken from her husband, film director **Blake Edwards**.

A welcome letter given out to patrons at the time reads in part, "**Julie Andrews Edwards** will only be signing books at today's event. She will not be able to sign memorabilia. Due to time constraints, **Julie Andrews Edwards** will not personalize your books today. She will only sign them. The taking of photographs is strictly prohibited at this event. Enjoy the signing!"

Well, despite all the restrictions, I had a great time. I had been thinking for days what I could possibly say to Julie. As I approached the desk, book extended, I said, "I have so many things I'd like to say to you, but I'll just say it's a pleasure to meet you."

To this, Julie, in her perfectly clipped British accent, replied, "It's a pleasure to meet you, too."

And with that, I was on my way.

I first met (to use the term loosely) **Ethel Merman**, often referred to as the first lady of the American musical stage, on July 25, 1970, the day I saw my first Broadway show, *Hello, Dolly!*

With a dozen hit shows behind her dating back to the 1930s, Miss Merman was nearing the end of her theatrical stage career. I am so fortunate to have been able to catch her before she took her final Broadway bow a few months later.

Miss Merman had been playing the title role since March of that year, following in the shoes and feathered hat of a long list of stars who had kept the show going into its seventh year, a record many at the time thought would never be broken.

I enjoyed the entire show, but I remember most vividly the scene in the Harmonia Gardens restaurant when Dolly was seated at a small round dining table downstage right, carving up some turkey for her intended, Horace Vandergelder. As she ate, she offered a bite or two to the theater patrons seated in the front row. How I wished she had done so to me, but as I was sitting up in row E, seat 111 of the balcony, that was not the least bit likely. Still, I loved how she broke that proverbial fourth wall, making me feel we were all in this together.

After the show, I waited for Miss Merman at the stage door. As I recall, she came out and headed straight for her waiting limousine, barely acknowledging the fans who had gathered on the sidewalk outside the St. James Theatre.

I walked up to the closed window of the limo and, with my Playbill in hand, indicated to Miss Merman that I wanted her to sign it for me. Through the glass she motioned to me, perhaps even mouthing the words, "I'm sorry," looking as if she really meant it, as the car joined the traffic heading off on 44th Street.

But this would not be the last time Miss Merman and I would come face to face. As you are finding out, I don't give up getting an autograph that easily. Years later, in 1978, Miss Merman wrote a book about her life, entitled simply, *Merman: An Autobiography*. Naturally, when I heard there was to be a book signing, I immediately planned to attend.

The exact date and place elude me, perhaps because I was otherwise preoccupied at the time . . . planning my approach. I was just two or three years out of school, working for pittance at a publishing company while awaiting an appointment to begin my teaching career, and money was tight. I knew I couldn't buy the book that day, but that wasn't what I was aiming for.

Armed with a couple of her old vinyl recordings, the original cast album of the Lincoln Center production of *Annie Get Your Gun* and one of her solo albums, "Ethel's Ridin' High," a collection of show tunes by the likes of **Cole Porter**, the **Gershwins**, and **Bock** & **Harnick**, which was released in 1974, I headed into the city, as we outer-borough residents refer to Manhattan.

The line was, not surprisingly, long, giving me ample time to review the situation and to figure out the best approach. I knew she wasn't supposed to sign any memorabilia, especially for anyone not buying the book, but I figured I would explain my predicament and hoped she would be sympathetic.

My turn finally arrived. I reached into my shopping bag and took out the two record covers (I would never bring along the actual records on excursions such as this). Not wanting anyone except Miss Merman to hear my story, I placed the albums on the L-shaped table in front of her, leaned over, and moved in a bit closer to her to whisper my explanation.

I don't think I got a single word out before that famous stentorian voice filled the entire department.

"Security! Security! This man is trying to get behind the table."

Within seconds, security was on the scene, assessing the situation. I, of course, was totally humiliated. Not only would everyone now know I wasn't buying the book, but I caused Broadway's biggest star to have a near breakdown.

"No, no," I assured her and the guards, whispering my explanation, "I can't buy the book today and I only wanted to ask Miss Merman to sign a couple of my records."

Everyone seemed to agree I posed no clear and present danger, and Miss Merman graciously signed both album covers. The writing implement of choice was a magic marker, not always the wisest option for writing on glossy covers. The "E" in Ethel, in fact, smeared on one of them, either at the time or sometime after that.

But I got my **Ethel Merman** autographs. It may have taken eight years, but mission finally accomplished.

the angel from brooklyn

By Paul DiSclafani (from "Long Island Living")

Every now and then, events happen that make you wonder if there really is a supreme being, or at least a Guardian Angel, looking out for you or your loved ones.

This story certainly puts that theory to the test. It's about a chance meeting at a gas station between an elderly woman (my mother) and a Good Samaritan stranger. It just so happens that he hailed from her old neighborhood in East New York.

Then again, maybe some people are just good-natured.

This column helped "Long Island Living" win First Place for the category "Narrative-Column" in the 2021 Press Club of Long Island Media Awards.

My mother didn't get her driver's license until she was about 40 years old. As a typical 1950's mom, she stayed home to take care of the children, the house, and nearly everything that didn't involve earning money. After the great migration to Long Island in the late '60s, most Brooklynites were now saddled with a mortgage. With my brother and me in school all day, my mother joined the workforce to help make ends meet.

After working locally down the block at Mays Department store, she took another job a few miles away (in Lindenhurst) that required transportation. She carpooled with a friend for a few months as a passenger, eventually making the decision to call a local driving instructor from down the block. There was no possible way my father was going to teach her how to drive. They would be divorced in less than three lessons.

My mother never learned how to ride a bicycle, yet she wanted to pilot a 2,000-pound vehicle. Her sense of direction was always a question mark, once getting lost just walking around our block. But she'd figured out how to get from Point A to Point B with two particular caveats; she doesn't drive on parkways, and she doesn't pump her own gas.

For 47 years, she has always found a station to pump her gas. Please understand that my mother needs gas about as often as a camel needs water. She has a 2013 Honda Civic with 7,000 miles on it. Most people log more than 1,000 miles a month, not a year.

Many gas stations used to offer "full" service, but unless you live in New Jersey, where all the stations pump gas for you, locating that today is as difficult as finding a payphone. I'll occasionally take her car and fill it (that lasts about three months), but sometimes she relies on strangers.

Recently, she stopped at a station on Merrick Road, where she had previous success with the clerk pumping the gas for her. She saw a man coming out and asked if he worked there. He had a kind face and told her that he had just gone in for a cup of coffee but asked if she needed help with something. Explaining her dilemma, he gladly offered to pump the gas for her.

She gave him $20 and asked if he could get $10 worth of gas for her.

"How do you know I won't just take your money?" he said with a sly smile on his face.

"I trust you," she said.

With that, he returned, handed her back the $10 change, asked if she would hold his coffee, then started pumping her gas.

Striking up a conversation, my mother was very appreciative and asked his name and where he was from.

"My name is Michael," he offered, "And I lived in the East New York section of Brooklyn for most of my life."

My mother is also from East New York, and it turns out they lived not too far from each other and knew a lot of the familiar landmarks.

While reminiscing together, she mentioned her grandson was also named Michael. He responded that he also had a son named Michael, and he was a police officer in Nassau County. What are the odds? Her Michael (my nephew) is also a Nassau County Police Officer!

She offered him a dollar for his time (he declined, of course), handed him back his coffee, and they went their separate ways. In the five minutes it took to put $10 gas into her car (a little more than three gallons at today's prices), my mother was convinced that this Michael was an Angel sent from heaven to help in her time of need.

Who knows, maybe he was...

the night the lights went out in brooklyn

By Paul DiSclafani (from "Long Island Living")

On the 40th Anniversary of the 1977 New York City Blackout, I read stories about the chaos that ensued. Long Islanders were spared as this was a Con Edison system issue, affecting only the five boroughs.

Almost 5,000 people were arrested for looting and general mayhem, with 550 police officers injured.

I thought about the first-ever blackout I had experienced as an 8-year-old in Brooklyn back in 1965 and remembered it was more fun than anything. The adults were sitting outside and partying while we kids enjoyed getting to play in the empty streets.

It was a different time, I guess.

July 13 marks the 40th anniversary of the blackout that paralyzed New York City in 1977.

On a hot, humid summer evening, a lightning strike at a substation on the Hudson River triggered havoc on the transmission lines. Following a series of mistakes and miscalculations, the entire Con Edison system shut down, forcing all of New York City into the darkness at 9:36 p.m. We here on Long Island were spared the plunge back into the dark ages thanks to our power company (remember LILCO?) being able to work their magic and keep our lines working.

Many businesses were already closed when complete darkness

hit. With people congregating outside to assess the situation, it created a perfect storm for the mayhem that was about to occur. The evening was about to morph into something even darker than New York City without any lights.

More than 4,500 people were arrested during the chaos that ensued, and more than 550 police officers were injured. The NYC Fire department put out 1,037 fires overnight while the citizens held their breath, waiting for daylight to arrive and break the spell. When the dust settled, more than 1,600 businesses had been damaged or destroyed.

Reliving the stories of turmoil during the Blackout of 1977 brought me back to the blackout I experienced as a kid in Brooklyn in November of 1965. Of course, everything that happened "back then" was better, or at least our memories of it are carefully crafted to remember only the good that came of it.

Back then, I took swimming lessons at the YMCA on Tuesday afternoons and would be picked up by a relative, whom I used to call Uncle Nick, around 5:30. My mother and brother would be at my Uncle Joe's house, where we would all meet up for dinner when my father came home.

While driving home with Uncle Nick, we got to a traffic light that wasn't working. It was unusual, but nothing to be alarmed about. Then he noticed all the streetlights were out, and by the time we completed the 10-minute drive, people were starting to mill around in the darkened streets, brandishing candles.

My mother and Aunt Faye, along with every other mother on the block, were in the middle of preparing dinner at 5:27 p.m. when the lights went out. Soon they were on the phone with other relatives, trying to confirm what seemed obvious; the lights were out all over the place.

Crazy talk of an alien attack was cool with us kids but seemed to be frightening the adults. As news reports of the blackout's cause began coming across the battery-operated radios, the initial shock of losing power began to wane.

It seemed power was out in the entire Northeast, but they expected to have it restored in a few hours. This reassuring news changed everything from a worrisome experience into a giddy, after-work gathering. We were way too young to know if alcohol was involved, but you can make your own assumptions.

There was a sense of camaraderie going on, at least in our little section of Brooklyn. Neighbors were sharing candles and helping each other get through the crisis, making the best of the situation. The blackout even sparked a light-hearted movie starring Doris Day called *Where Were You When the Lights Went Out?*

Thirty million people in eight states in the Northeast, roughly 80,000 square miles, were out of power for up to 13 hours. Brooklyn got power back sometime after 11:00 p.m. that night. Most people who faced that blackout think of it fondly as a happening they will never forget.

Many of our parents' generation grew up without a dependency on electricity, so maybe that's why there was no widespread panic. This was their "back then."

That night, across the five boroughs, New York recorded the lowest amount of crime on any night in documented history. Only five people were arrested for looting, and there was no property damage reported. I guess people stayed home and made the best of the situation.

And curiously enough, nine months later, the number of live births was higher than expected...

3 days in october

by Mark Fleisher

Growing up in the Brooklyn, New York, of the 1940s and 1950s meant my love and loyalty were with the Dodgers. The Boys of Summer were my heroes. "Dem Bums" as they were affectionately called, could raise your spirits, then break your heart – all in the same baseball season. That feature led to the title of my unfinished and barely started boyhood memoir titled "I Died Twice Before Age 15."

My initial demise came on October 3, 1951, when the Dodgers faced the arch rival New York Giants in the third game of a best-of-three playoff for the National League pennant and the right to reach the World Series. The teams were tied one game apiece after the Dodgers blew a 13 1/2-game lead during the regular season. Brooklyn led the Giants 4-1 entering the ninth inning of the deciding playoff game. New York scored once, then off the bat of Bobby Thomson -- "The Flying Scot" -- came "The Shot Heard 'Round the World," a three-run walk-off home run into the Polo Grounds' short left-field porch on a pitch from the scarred-for-life Ralph Branca. This eight-year-old and the Borough of Brooklyn descended into dark despair, growing darker each time we heard the shriek of Giants' announcer Russ Hodges – "the Giants win the pennant, the Giants win the pennant."

Wounds festered half a century later with the revelation that the Giants employed an elaborate but illegal sign-stealing operation to make up ground during the regular season. Thomson swore the system was not used when he hit the fateful home run, but cheating clearly aided the Giants bid to draw even with the Dodgers at season's end.

Resurrection, albeit temporary, came four years later on October 4, 1955, when the Dodgers defeated the New York Yankees for their first and only World Series championship in Brooklyn. A stunning catch by Sandy Amoros and the brilliant pitching of young lefthander Johnny Podres clinched the seventh and deciding game, triggering a tumultuous celebration among the faithful when shortstop Pee Wee Reese fielded Elston Howard's grounder and threw across the diamond to first baseman Gil Hodges for the final out.

The revelry lasted two more seasons before Dodgers' owner Walter O'Malley delivered the coup de grace. On October 8, 1957, he announced the abandonment of Brooklyn for the Left Coast, specifically a stadium located in something called Chavez Ravine in Los Angeles. The Boys of Summer -- My Boys of Summer -- headed to La-La Land! In the eyes of Brooklyn fans, O'Malley joined Adolf Hitler and Joseph Stalin as the three most hated men of the 20th Century.

I could not bring myself to root for the Dodgers of Los Angeles. The Yankees? Never. Besides, I wanted to stay in the National League – the senior circuit as Red Barber would say.

I settled on St. Louis. Why the Cardinals? Primarily because of Stan Musial. Although the Cards were "the enemy" of the Dodgers, Musial almost always was greeted with applause – if merely polite – when he stepped into the batter's box and untwisted that corkscrew swing that made him arguably the best left-handed hitter of his day. (Sorry, Ted Williams). I guess the Ebbets Field fans appreciated his style, grace, and talent as much as I did.

I chose the Cards even though right-handed pitcher Gerry Staley had verbally brushed me aside with a "don't bother me, kid" as my Dad and I and Staley walked from a nearby subway stop to the ball park one day in the early 1950s. I guess Musial and his mates in those first years of fandom – McCarver, Mizell, and Moon; Boyer and Blasingame; Flood; and Gibson – atoned for Staley's slight.

Forgiveness came with age and some years later I decided it was time for reconciliation and I began rooting for the Los Angeles Dodgers, if not with the degree of fervor when they occupied Ebbets Field.

The connection strengthened when I first visited Albuquerque, New Mexico, in 2010 and in 2013 when I moved permanently to the Land of Enchantment. The Triple-A Albuquerque Isotopes were the Dodgers' farm team in the Pacific Coast League. (Did I mention the PCL is headed by Branch Rickey III, grandson of Branch Rickey who broke baseball's color barrier when he brought Jackie Robinson to Brooklyn in 1947?)

As luck would have it, ties between Los Angeles and Albuquerque soon ended when the Dodgers moved their Triple-A affiliate to Oklahoma City. The Colorado Rockies quickly filled the void in Albuquerque. It wasn't the same for me, but at least Triple-A ball continued.

And it proved once again, the Dodgers could break your heart whether they resided in Brooklyn or Los Angeles.

a stay at the algonquin hotel

By Suzanne Kamata

My daughter's first question upon checking into the Algonquin Hotel near Times Square in New York City is "Do they have Wi-Fi here?"

As for me, I glance around the dark wooded tables of the Round Table restaurant, eager to channel past visitors through less modern means. Perhaps the ghost of one-time resident legendary actor John Barrymore is here, or the spirits of the rapier-witted writer Dorothy Parker, who worked a couple of streets over at the offices of *Vogue* and *Vanity Fair*, or Pulitzer Prize winner Edna Ferber, who penned *Showboat* and *Giant*, among other successful novels and screenplays. The latter two were part of the so-called Vicious Circle, a.k.a. the Round Table, a group of writers and critics who met for lunch and barbed banter in the hotel's lobby restaurant for ten years. The group became a literary legend. Even President John F. Kennedy once said that he dreamed of being part of the "ten-year lunch at the Algonquin." Just before the elevator arrives, I snap a photo of the painting of the original Round Table members which hangs over the area where they were said to dine.

We take our bags up to the ninth floor. The walls in the corridor are hung with posters of vintage *New Yorker* covers and cartoons. Editor Harold Ross raised money to launch the prestigious magazine here, making him part of Algonquin lore. Each door is hung with a framed quote by a Round Table member. Our room, just around the corner from the marble staircase with its filigreed black cast iron railing, features the words of writer Robert Benchley: "Anyone can do any amount of work provided it isn't the work he is supposed to be doing at the moment." Indeed.

Although the hotel dates back to 1902, making it the longest continuously running hotel in New York City, it is now equipped with all of the modern amenities, including a fitness center. I open the door with a key card to a well-appointed room with a flat-screen TV, the latest copy of the *New Yorker*, and, yes, free Wi-Fi. "The Gonk," as the hotel is affectionately nicknamed, also has a cat, which we haven't yet encountered.

The following morning I descend to the Blue Bar adjacent to the lobby where "prohibition-style" cocktails are served in the evening. At night, the room is illuminated with blue bulbs which are said to cast a flattering light in accordance with John Barrymore's declaration that Broadway players preferred complexion-enhancing blue tones onstage. Framed caricatures of famous New Yorkers by Al Hirsch, a renowned artist himself, add to the ambiance.

During the day, the Blue Bar is where hotel guests line up to get their morning coffee. As I stand behind another woman waiting for my complimentary beverage, I ask her if she's seen the cat.

She smiles. "Last I saw him, he was in the window."

I nod, resisting the urge to correct her. It's a she. Her name is Matilda. She's a purebred Ragdoll with her own Facebook page and Twitter feed. Every year the hotel holds a birthday party for her, at which there is a cat fashion show and a charity auction. To be fair, I only learned about Matilda recently myself from the picture book *Matilda, the Algonquin Cat*, written by Leslie Martini, and illustrated by Massimo Mongiardo, whose artwork was inspired by that on the Round Table's menus.

The current Matilda is the latest in a long line of cats, beginning with a stray brought in by Barrymore in the 1930s and named Hamlet. Ever since then, the hotel has had a feline in residence. The males have all been named Hamlet, while the females have always been called Matilda.

Cup of coffee in hand, I step out onto the sidewalk and see a ball of fluffy gray fur curled up in the window in her special cat house. Matilda is sleeping. A sign pleads that visitors do not tap on the glass to get her attention. Although I want to see her face, I don't try to wake her.

The Algonquin Hotel is smack in the theater district, and in walking distance of a variety of shops and restaurants. My daughter and I go around the block to try out the famous cheesecake at Junior's. On the way we pass food carts selling halal hot dogs, T-shirt vendors, and the notorious Naked Cowboy, strumming a guitar in underpants. Later, we visit a bookstore on Fifth Avenue, and take in a musical at the Minskoff Theater. When we return to the hotel, Matilda is again sleeping in the window, but this time we can see her sweet face and catch a glimpse of her rhinestone collar.

Dorothy Parker wrote, "New York is always a little more than you had hoped for." I imagine that the ghost of animal-lover Parker is lingering somewhere nearby, admiring her as well.

old neighborhood (1970's)

By Lisa Diaz Meyer

I could tell it was an old neighborhood as I sat on the fire escape. There wasn't much action below; just a few children playing games. The dilapidated cars in the streets were parked in regimental formation. Houses, old and broken, looked as if life were non-existent, yet through darkened windows, the clotheslines draped white bedding. The streets were lined with rusted garbage cans twisted and bent with abuse.

    From behind a tree a man appeared, approaching the apartment building. At first, I did not see him coming; it was the sounds of newly purchased shoes hitting the wet sidewalk that attracted my attention. His face and movements were drained of all delight. I recognized him to be the landlord who has lived here most of his life.

a weekend in new york

by Richard Harries

Never wanted to go to New York
Don't often go to big cities
I had heard of the high crime rate
In news, drama, even a musical or two
So it had never appealed

From work an offer of a charter flight
No interest to me
Then it was announced that my favourite
Petula Clark was to open on Broadway
In Blood Brothers with David and Shaun Cassidy

So out of the bin the leaflet came and off I went
A long, for me, flight
But in those days drink and food on the plane we're plentiful
Packed light as it was only a weekend
Landed on time in JFK
Snow was everywhere that November

To the hotel off Times Square
Had a nap then off for a meal
Everywhere seemed bright and clean
Staff were friendly, but no food to be seen

So off we went to a cafe bar

Reminded me of CHEERS
We ate and drank and I found out
What eggs over easy were
Coffee galore and the waitress filled my cup
As soon as it was empty

Asked for the bill, she said 'You mean the tab?'
Asked what we had had, menu number 2
And many coffees, I did not know how many
'You had one, I just refilled it'
Wow everythings so cheap here in New York

Off to the theatre, transfixed
A full house and they smashed it
A good night's rest then my companion
Decided he had jet lag and went to sleep
So off I went on my own and explored

Discovered local taxes, something I did not know about
So a ten dollar T-shirt for my daughter
Was $12.50, a surprise
Wandered around saw ice skating at the Rockefeller Centre
But did not join in, just loved watching

Found myself at the return ticket booth
In Times Square. I meant to see something else
I truly did, but a Blood Brothers ticket was returned
So off to the matinee with Petula
And again, I loved it

Then on to the Texas Steakhouse, with new friends
So four of us ordered. I asked for beer
A four pint pitcher arrived
I said I only wanted a pint, but this was all mine

About to return to the theatre so no way!

Ordered a steak, told to get food from the salad bar
Not all lettuce like in the UK but crab and prawns and more
Vast plate filled up and eaten, delicious
Then the steak arrived, so large
Looked like half a dead cow on a plate

Never seen anything so vast
Compared to London it was all so cheap
Back to the theatre for the evening show
Stopping on the way at Macy's,
Presents for family back home

Everywhere was wonderful and vibrant
And I realised I loved the place
I wanted to be there
The city had won my heart
I had only expected to love the show!

Next day madness, dashing around
Seeing the sights and then the flight
All so brief, a whirlwind tour
And the musical three times
In just a weekend

New York had won, truly won my heart

my second trip to blood brothers (petula and broadway)

By Richard Harries

So I booked a cheap flight
Went to New York through the night
To see BLOOD BROTHERS again
My enthusiasm did not wane
New York was an amazing place
Lots of adventures, put a smile on my face
The performance was absolutely great
I did the production totally rate
As the best thing I had ever seen
Beyond anything I ever could dream
David and Shaun Cassidy excelled
At Petula's desolation my tears welled
For her it was the perfect part
What genius she displayed in her art!
She invited us into her dressing room
My heart did zing and zoom!
She was so sweet and full of grace
Talking one to one with her was ace
We had booked to see the show twice
But on Saturday afternoon I was left to my own device
Wandered to the remaindered booth in Times Square
And at the other shows titles did stare
Then a ticket for BLOOD BROTHERS was returned

And my heart did leap and I yearned
To see the show for a third time
And soon that ticket was mine
As I came out onto the street
My heart did jump and beat
As a big boom microphone was thrust in my face
And a TV reporter with camera invaded my space
She said 'Which show did you get a ticket to see'
'I replied 'BLOOD BROTHERS I did, me'
'A Limey! You've come a long way
Surely not just to see this show today?'
'Not at all said I'
With a sigh
'I came to see Petula Clark
In something so modern and dark'
'Now why did SHE get the part?'
'Well she is a great actress that's a start.
She has made over 30 films and been in plays divine'
'So she has paid her dues, that's fine'
Said the reporter to me
With typical American glee
Can you by any chance
And she gave me an encouraging glance
Name any of her hits at all?'
I tried not to laugh and then fall

Would you like them in date order or should
I list them alphabetically (as I could)

She looked at me aghast
I started early and got to KISS ME GOODBYE at last

'CUT' shouted the reporter, thanked me and then fled
Looking at me kind of strange with dread

So I guess that somewhere on American TV
Will be shown clips of foreign eccentrics, including me!

take me back to brooklyn, please

by Mark Fleisher

Take me back to Brooklyn, please
where I delight in a Coney Island breeze
Jackie and Gil, Duke, Pee Wee and Roy
so many heroes for this Brooklyn boy
Take me back to Brooklyn, please
where I delight in a Coney Island breeze
My pals and I bled Dodger blue
loyal in victory and in defeat, too
But the team we loved the very most
deserted us for the other coast
When the Boys of Summer took their leave
the Flatbush Faithful had cause to grieve
Take me back to Brooklyn, please
where I delight in a Coney Island breeze
Boys on the corner under a street light
singing do-wop all through a summer night
We feasted on pizza at 15 cents a slice
savoring the cheese and sauce and spice
A kosher hot dog and a Doctor Brown's
tastes to wipe away all our frowns
Take me back to Brooklyn, please
where I delight in a Coney Island breeze
Strolling the Promenade in Brooklyn Heights

absorbing all the sounds, smells and sights
Manhattan, Williamsburg, Brooklyn – bridges three
no tolls extracted, cross them all for free
Take me back to Brooklyn, please
where I delight in a Coney Island breeze
Those days created lasting memories
and now I bask in such sweet reveries
So take me back to Brooklyn, please
where I delight in a Coney Island breeze

i am from …

by Jim Tritten

I am from … a time and a New York that no longer exists,
    It used to exist … but most of us who could remember that time no longer are here,
    Or can no longer remember,
    It was a time of growth as I learned what it would take to move forward …
    … and adjust with time as it advanced,
    It was a time of safety nurtured by loving immigrant grandparents,
    A grandmother who could cook toast, Hungarian *huluska*, and chicken …
    … better than I have ever experienced anywhere since,
    And a grandfather who took me to Ebbets Field to watch the Brooklyn Dodgers,
    … curses on anyone that celebrated their ignominious move the LA-LA-Land,
    It was the time of my first girlfriends,
    Girlfriends because at the age of six, I had two,
    My mother asked me what we should name my new sister,
    That's how my sister became Susan Janet,
    It was a time to make lifelong friends and never worry about their politics,

It was a time to stretch and explore the whole city on the subway for ten cents,

... and sail on the Steamship Alexander Hamilton up the Hudson,

I earned the rank of Eagle Scout and am still proud of that achievement,

I had great scout leaders who served as excellent role models,

We went upstate to Boy Scout summer camp,

... and experienced what New York was like before the first contact,

It was a time to learn that giving back and sharing was not just expected ...

... but good for society,

I learned about karma later,

I am from a time when a President spoke to us and said not to ask what your country can do for you ...

... but what you can do for your country,

I am from a time when volunteering for the military was expected ... appreciated ... and something to be proud of,

I am from a time when those who had other opinions about the military threw raw eggs on my uniform ...

... when I was stationed at Floyd Bennett Field in Brooklyn ... and visiting campuses on recruiting visits,

I am from a time when no one ever said ... "Thank you for your service,"

I am from a time when everyone I knew used racial and ethnic slurs,

I am from a time when many things taken for granted today were illegal,

... as were many things that we are being told are now the new normal,

I am from a time when I ate mustard sandwiches because we could not afford baloney,

I am from ... a time ... and a New York ... that no longer exists.

this town

by Jordan M Frazier

This town is full of dreamers
This town is full of losers
Hear them cry in the alleyways
This town has hope in the young
This town has care for the old
This is the town where anything goes
You can love a man, or you can love a women
Or you can love anything that can love in return
This is the town of many generations, one that has seen war, one that has seen the rise of music, one that has seen terror and the one just born
This town has endured war and hardship with its people tired and sick
This town has celebrated Christmas many times over
Over the years you may sit, and wonder is there any more magic left in this old town
People come and go
As all things pass and come to an end
This town has seen it all over the years
The Good and The Bad, love and loss
But you can still hear in the silence and the echoes
The homecoming is here
So, celebrate this old town

that awakens with the sleepless city

by Katrenia Busch

Keep mine eye upon the city,
Where it's said to never sleep—
Let mine eyes rest not nor ever see
Time and times that they can't keep

Let mine footprints travel much and far,
Throughout this sleepless city—
That mine eyes search first ahead and are
Always leading my feet before me!

Let mine breath be born each day,
From the city's fast paced means
That is of course to say—
Let the air of the city— be what I breathe

Let mine voice be heard— perceived
Whether by silence or word and words
That awakens with this sleepless city—
That we have known as New York

the little book that did

by Mark Fleisher

I don't own a Kindle
I don't possess a Nook
When it comes to reading
I prefer to hold a book

It was a small book, inconsequential in size. Twelve pages, maybe twenty, certainly no more. Yet *The Little Engine That Could* meant the world to me when Mrs. Bernthal, my first grade teacher, presented it to me at the end of the school year at Public School 219. I don't remember why she chose me nor do I remember the inscription she wrote – something about being a good reader, I think.

Little did I know this book would launch a lifetime of reading and, in time, writing.

Like most boys growing up in Brooklyn, New York during the 1940s and 1950s I was a sports fanatic. I graduated from the Little Engine to the sports-oriented novels of John R. Tunis whose words stoked my athletic fires.

New York in those years was a city with a multitude of daily newspapers. Tabloids numbered the Daily News, Daily Mirror the Post. Full-size newspapers – called broadsheets – included

The Times, Herald Tribune, World-Telegram and Sun and the Journal-American. Brooklyn had its own newspaper, the Eagle, until its demise in 1955.

The Times, Daily News and World-Telegram were my family's popular dailies. I read them voraciously devouring the sports pages before heading to news accounts from around the world. One reason, I suppose, we didn't own a television and the papers along with a multi-band Pilot radio were our sources of information.

My dad was a postal employee, mostly working nights at the Post Office adjacent to Grand Central Station in midtown Manhattan. He moonlighted some weekends helping a friend run a newsstand on Broadway at the corner of West 50th Street. Dad got to know the doorman at the nearby Capitol Theater. I'd often take the subway into Manhattan, meet my father and we'd go to the Capitol. The price of admission: a good cigar for the friendly doorman. In those days, many of the theaters had stage shows in addition to a first run movie. I recall performances by singers Johnny Ray and Georgia Gibbs among others.

Dad would arrive home Sunday with bundles of the day's papers bound with thick twine. No wonder my dad had very muscular arms! I made sure I had my homework done so I could spend the hours before bed reading most every word.

He sometimes frequented the out-of-town and international newspaper stand in Times Square. Dad often brought home issues of the London Times and Manchester Weekly Guardian printed on what seemed like tissue paper. Who cared if the papers were several days old?

As I entered my teens newspapers began to take second place behind books. At my dad's suggestion I read *Penrod* by Booth Tarkington and the *Lanny Budd* series by Upton Sinclair, the famed muckraker and political activist. Soon Hemingway and Thomas Wolfe found room on my bookshelf.

The used book stores along Fourth Avenue in Manhattan became a haven for almost any genre you might imagine. I spent many a Saturday afternoon thumbing through the books on sidewalk tables or reconnoitering the musty shelves for literary treasures or oddities. Nearby at the corner of Fifth Avenue and East 18th Street stood the Parthenon of Book Stores – the original Barnes and Noble – a multi-storied edifice with each floor brimming with tables and shelves of you-name-it, they had it.

Sojourns to the Fourth Avenue stores and Barnes and Noble brought about my "Russian Period" where I gobbled up editions of Tolstoy, Pushkin, Gogol, Chekhov and Dostoevsky.

One summer vacation I stumbled into what I thought would be the perfect job – working in a book store near Brooklyn College. Alas, the experience turned out to be menial and tedious. My responsibility was in the basement, putting together steel shelving to hold the overflow of books. When the boss wasn't looking I'd sneak upstairs, eyeball a book I wanted, and hide it before a customer beat me to the punch.

Time to speed up the tape and talk about current days.

I've gravitated to primarily reading non-fiction, mainly American history. But I cop to reading escapist literature, especially during the pandemic and other perilous days. Nothing like a good police procedural or John le Carre' spy novel to channel the mind away from the crisis du jour.

There's no telling what might inhabit my bookshelves or bedside table. I hope at least one of my six poetry books finds a home with a friend or acquaintance. I've enjoyed this journey, partnering with books these many years. And to think it all started with the *Little Engine That Could*.

fated meeting in nyc

By Janet Metz Walter

I was lying in bed in semi darkness, staring at the ceiling. As if I was watching a movie on a screen, visions played in my head and transferred themselves onto the ceiling. They weren't just visions, they were memories from childhood.

A chance encounter on a street in New York City had awakened those memories and provided so many more, I became lost in fantasy.

As a child I lived in a newly built complex of three story apartment buildings. There were 10 apartments on each floor, most of them occupied by young families who heralded the start of the "Baby Boomer" generation. Many of the fathers were young men who had served in the military during the recently ended WWII and were now starting new jobs and new families. It was a good place to start out. There were children to play with and neighbors to chat with. There were courtyards to sit in and stores within walking distance for new mothers, most of whom did not drive. The men had other men to swap stories with, and play sports or cards together. My father found guys to play Racquetball with down at the nearby park. My mother met neighbors while walking with me and my brother in the stroller.

I started school and had friends to play with, but each year I had a fewer friends as the kids learned to ride bikes, and roller skate and play sports, and I got left behind because I unfortunately was grievously uncoordinated and lacked the ability to ride or keep up with the skaters or runners.

I gained weight and retreated into shyness. My mother bought my dresses in the Chubby Department of Macy's. There must have been other chubby kids if Macy's had a Chubby Department, but kids started to say things, mostly kids in school who lived in the neighborhoods surrounding the school.

As typical kids we sometimes got into arguments, but the first one that I remember is when Amy Kruger moved in. We had the same name, except my name is spelled Aimee. My mother thought it was different, sophisticated and pretty. One day when we were drawing, Amy saw a paper with my name on it, Aimee Segal.

"That's not how you spell Amy," she informed me.

"That's how I spell it", I told her, but she insisted that my name was Aaameee. I went home and tearfully told my mother that she had spelled my name wrong. Mom told me that lots of names are spelled in many different ways: Steven could be spelled with a "v" or a "ph." Eileen could be spelled "Eileen" or "Ilene."

I realized she was right, but Amy kept calling me Aaameee.

My mother very rarely interfered in these little issues but she finally decided that she would have to have a chat with Amy's mother. Then of course Amy raged at me that I was a tattletale. I decided to keep away from her as much as possible. She managed to find a couple of other mean girls to hang out with. By the time sixth grade rolled around I knew almost every kid in the class, both from Parkwood Apartments where I lived, and from the surrounding neighborhood.

Diana Young and I became good friends fairly quickly. She was cute, and very sweet. She didn't seem to have a mean bone in her body. It was quite a coincidence that Steven Rubin, my next door neighbor, wound up sitting next to Diana, and a new boy in the neighborhood, Nick Donato, sat next to me.

As the term wore on, hormones started slowly kicking in, I grew a little bit and lost a little of the baby fat. I could now get my clothes from the regular children's department. I got a little more comfortable around Nick, and some of the other boys in the class, although I was still very shy and it was still difficult.

As the year was drawing to an end, the next thing to become nervous about was Junior High School, as what is now Middle School was called in those days. There we would be joined by a whole group of new kids from other schools.

About two weeks before school ended I received a surprise invitation to a graduation party. My mother was friendly with Kate Castle who lived a few blocks away from us in a private house. I knew her twins, Jessica and Joshua, and had occasional play dates with Jessica. Josh had his own friends, and I didn't see much of him. He was blonder, but he looked a lot like Jessica.

The twins decided that they would like to have a party, and Kate thought it was a great idea. I have no idea if it was Jessica's idea to invite me, or her mother's but I received an invitation for a Friday evening at their house. I wasn't sure I wanted to go.

Even though we were in the same grade, the twins' birthday was in the middle of January, and they were among the oldest in the class, and my birthday was December 18 and I was the youngest. The 11 months made quite a difference in our maturity.

One of the girls who was invited to the party informed me that her mother was letting her wear stockings, and that most of the girls were wearing them.

Stockings were what women wore then, two stockings held up by garters. Pantyhose would not be invented and sold until the following year.

I told my mother that the girls were wearing stockings. She told me I was too young and that she would not let me wear them. So I wore Mary Janes with blue socks. I looked and felt like a baby, not a girl entering Junior High. Some of the girls looked at me and whispered to each other. Barbara Harmon, the only girl from my class waved at me and I joined her on a chair in the corner. At least I had someone to talk to. There were about eight girls and six boys. There was music playing from the record player. A stack of 45's were loaded onto the spindle. Some of the girls started dancing with each other. Some boys asked girls to dance. Mark Lewis asked Barbara to dance. I sat in my corner watching.

Josh came over to me. I don't know if he came on his own or if his mother sent him over. I'm sure she did not want my mother to find out that I sat in a corner all night. "Would you like to dance?" he asked.

Confused and embarrassed, afraid that I would be embarrassing him I said "You don't have to dance with me."

"And you don't have to sit in a corner all night"

He held out his hand. The Everly Brothers were singing "All I Have To Do Is Dream." It was a Cha-Cha. My father, who was a great dancer, had taught me how to do it. I started to dance and Josh said to me "I'm not very good at this. I never really learned it."

I stood next to him and started teaching him the steps.

For the moment I forgot my discomfort as I worked the steps with him. He seemed to be pleased. He didn't seem uncomfortable at all.

"I think Gina is mad," I whispered to Josh.

He shrugged his shoulders. "I'm dancing with you now."

"Tequila" came on and Jessica pulled me over to dance with the girls. Josh had been very nice to me. I still wondered whether he had been told to dance with me. I was still a caterpillar who had some changes to go through in my cocoon.

In Junior High I met the kids that had gone to the other schools in the area. For the most part the kids from Parkwood still stuck together.

Afternoons after school were spent watching "American Bandstand" and teaching myself how to dance like the kids on the show.

The twins' party had put a little crack in my painful shyness. I had gotten a bagful of hand-me-downs from an older, very stylish cousin and I was dressing like all the other girls. The caterpillar was slowly changing inside her cocoon.

High School was a whole other story - or many stories. The

butterfly emerged from the cocoon rather suddenly and had to learn how to fly. It was not always an easy flight. Not all the flowers I landed on were sweet smelling, but I slowly learned the ropes of socializing, dating, dealing with old friends and new friends, in groups and separately.

It was interesting, memorable and life changing.

I had hardly seen Josh through most of High School. He was not in any of my classes, and we waved in the hallways occasionally, but I ran into his friend Paul, who was already in college, at a fraternity party and we went out a few times. I decided to ask him to the prom since I was comfortable with him and he knew most of my friends. I wasn't sure he would accept, but I think he was excited about spending time with old friends and he told me he would be happy to go with me.

The prom was at a catering hall that was part of a beach club. Everyone was invited back to spend the day at the beach the next day.

It was a happy/sad time. People were saying goodbye to their friends who were going away to college. It was an uncertain time. President Kennedy's picture was the frontispiece page of our yearbook. He had been assassinated only 7 months ago.

A war in Korea had ended and a war in Viet Nam was beckoning. Guys were going from graduation into the Military. But it was still Prom night.

Paul and I danced a little and hung out with friends.

A Cha-Cha came on. Before I knew it, Josh was at my side.

"How about a dance for old times sake."

I looked at Paul and he smiled and waved me on. It had been six years since that awkward night in the sixth grade. Josh looked good. He played Tennis and had a golden tan. I tried not to show it but I was kind of tingly.

I had changed a lot. My face was the same but my body had matured. My face was enhanced by the makeup I wore.

Most of all, I wasn't the shy, immature kid that I had been in sixth grade.

We talked a little small talk while we were dancing and then he dropped the bomb. His father had taken a job in Seattle and had been there for two months. He was just waiting for the twins to graduate to bring them and Kate out there.

I had been expecting him to say that he was going away to college but this was really going away. It wasn't that I had spent time with him through High School but I felt a little sad that they were all leaving.

"Jessica is still a little shell shocked," he told me. "I'm sure she would have told you sometime tonight or tomorrow."

He gave me a hug and said he hoped to see me tomorrow. I wished him luck, in case he didn't. The next day was fun and relaxing.

Jessica and I shed a few tears of goodbye and good luck. Josh hugged me again, a tight hug enfolded in his arms.

College was local. Social life consisted of going to discos, and dances at hotels and catering halls, run by a singles organization. There were no cell phones, no swiping left or right to reject someone or be rejected, no dating sites.

It was up close and personal.

There were girls in school who were already married. The war in Vietnam was in full swing and guys who were married, at least at that moment in time avoided the draft.

I met Jon Davidoff in September of my Junior year, in my English class. He was a little reserved but he had a good sense of humor.

By the New Year we were officially considered a couple. He proposed in a park on July 4 under a canopy of fireworks over a nearby lake.

By the time we were married five years we had two children.

Business had its ups and downs. Life had its ups and downs. The years rolled by. It was a Friday in May 2004. Out of our whole group from High School the one I had remained most friendly with was Fran Aaronson. She lived a few miles away from me, but also had an apartment in the city where she spent most weekends. Her daughter lived in the city. Jon was away on a quick trip to DC and due to come home the next afternoon. Fran and I decided to get together and go to The Tenement Museum. She had never been there. I made reservations online and got an email confirmation.

I was going to park in a lot near Fran's midtown apartment.

While I was driving I got a frantic call from Fran. Her grandson had slammed a door on his finger and she had to take care of her other grandson while her daughter took the injured one to the Emergency Room to see if the finger was broken.

The day was sunny and warm, but not hot. I was already driving and I had paid for the tickets, so I decided to go by myself and try to sell the other ticket when I got to the museum. It was only noon and I had some time to kill.

I was disappointed, but it turned out to be absolute fate! I parked in the lot and planned to take a cab down to the museum.

As I was walking to the corner, a man walked out of the hotel that was on the corner of the street. The hair was true salt and pepper, light brown and silver mingled together. The face was older but I knew it was Josh!

His physique was still basically the same. He was dressed in jeans and a light grey long sleeve button down shirt. The sleeves were rolled up.

I stopped for a minute to stare at him and he looked at me and said, "Aimee?" I guess I hadn't changed all that much.

And so, Fate was sealed.

The whole thing took me a minute to process. He moved toward me and we hugged. "What are you doing here?" I stammered. "Is your family with you?"

He was here to attend a trade show at the Javits Center that had just ended. He had been here since Sunday and was flying home tomorrow. He was alone.

He had visited family on Sunday night, and gotten together with friends on Tuesday night. Now his plan was to go see The Intrepid.

I didn't have to think twice. His hug told me that he was happy to see me. "How set are you on doing that?" I asked.

He looked at me quizzically.

I explained what had happened with Fran, and that I had this extra ticket. It would be a nice time to catch up if he wanted to join me.

"Wow, my grandfather grew up on the Lower East Side. I think I would really enjoy doing that." His immediate answer surprised me a little.

In the cab we started to catch up.

He develops software for children's games. Not too astounding for someone from Seattle.

He told me about his family and his son who was getting divorced and has a young son for whom Josh and his wife often babysat.

Jessica actually married another twin, and although it is supposed to skip a generation, she has a son and twin daughters. I gave him back the same information about Jon, my kids and grandkids. We skirted the edges of Chinatown and arrived at the museum. The Lower East Side is almost like a different country compared to the rest of the city.

The apartment building now housing the museum was built in 1863. There are some apartment buildings that were built in the 1970's.

When Josh saw the street sign "Orchard Street," he exclaimed "Oh, I remember my mother taking us shopping here when we were kids!"

"I think we may have come here together once," I told him.

"It's not like I remember it," he mused.

Orchard Street had indeed changed. When we came here as kids it was like a huge flea market. One shop after another with clothing on racks outside the shops and more racks jammed inside, with wall to wall people jammed among the racks.

My mom had bought me my first leather jacket here, red, when I was about 12 years old. Now many of the shops had been replaced with apartment buildings, some restaurants, and regular stores. Very little of the chaos that made the street so fascinating in the 60's remained. The entrance into the museum is through the gift shop.

"Wow!" Josh exclaimed. "I was wondering where I would find gifts to bring home for Carol and the kids."

He started browsing books, games, and pocketbooks. We bought gifts and left them with the cashier for pick up after the tour.

The first tour was of the apartment of garment workers who worked and lived in a 325 sq foot apartment. It is mind boggling the way people lived and managed in those days. There were about five people who lived in that apartment.

Our generation, and especially our kids, had no idea what we have to appreciate. The second tour was of an apartment that was divided into three parts to show who lived there after WWII. We were told the stories of a Jewish family, a Hispanic family and a Chinese family. It was also very informative and fascinating.

At the end of the tour we picked up our bags and wandered outside. While Josh was checking out I had called Tina. She told me that her grandson's finger was badly bruised but not broken. I briefly told her about meeting Josh.

'We're going to have to have a long talk tomorrow!"

I told her we absolutely would.

It was a little early for dinner so we walked and talked, about old classmates, about our lives. He met his wife through a mutual friend and they were married about two years after I was. He was so pleasant I was wondering if he was showing me his "work face," but he told me he dealt with kids a lot when they were testing the software and he was just a chill type of guy. We both were out of our regular environment and it was like a vacation. All the tensions of work, and home and family had just faded away. We were in our own little bubble.

We were deciding what to do for dinner. Josh said that whenever he came to New York he tried to go to a New York Deli since that was what he missed in Seattle.

That was a piece of cake. Katz's Deli was right around the corner.

"Are you sure I'm not keeping you from packing or something?" Vestiges of my childhood anxieties coming out.

"What's the matter?" he asked with a mock sigh. "Are you getting sick of me already?" "Not at all," I smiled back. "Just trying to be polite."

"Well here's the deal," he had raised his voice just a notch.

"Number 1: Neither of us had lunch and we agreed to eat dinner together in any case."

"Number 2: My plane doesn't leave until three tomorrow, and I am mostly packed so I have plenty of time, and.."

"Number 3 : I am paying for dinner since you paid for the museum tickets. That is not negotiable!"

I started to giggle. The assertive side of Josh was finally coming out.

It was early for dinner, only 5:25, but we still had to wait ten minutes for a table. The place was crowded and noisy. It had a distinctive smell of pickled meats and pickles, and cases of pastries by the registers.

There were counters for take out where waiters were shouting orders for sandwiches. A woman at the next table sent back her soup because it was cold.

The guy behind us who was obviously a tourist with a deep Southern accent asked the waiter what a Kasha Knish was.

Sitting with our corned beef sandwiches and potato knishes, Josh swirled the ice in his soda with his straw, as he told me about his son Lenny and his grandson Charlie.

Lenny had married pretty young, at the age of 24. Charlie was born a year later. Lenny was an Accountant and his wife Terri was an evening Production Assistant at a TV news station.

Basically Charlie was taken care of, but she and Lenny never saw each other, especially during tax season when Lenny was working overtime every day. They just grew apart and when Charlie was finally in school full time they decided to end it.

Josh and Carole and Terri's parents helped take care of Charlie.

"I'm sorry I brought the mood down," Josh said between bites, "But I feel so comfortable talking to you."

"Well I've waited a long time to pay you back for dancing with me at that party," I answered smiling, trying to lighten the mood.

He chuckled and we turned our attention back to old friends, and travel stories and commenting on the variety show that was going on all around us in the restaurant.

Finally he asked "Do you have anything that you are doing this evening?' I looked at him and my antenna went up. What was he thinking? I kept my face composed.

"Why? What are you thinking?" My guard was up.

He leaned back against the seat and looked at me.

"You look like a deer in the headlights!"

"No I don't," I countered, but I could feel myself starting to blush.

"Maybe a mouse being stalked by a cat."

He chuckled. "Have you ever known me to be a bad boy?"

"Ummm, I haven't seen you in 40 years."

Just the sound of it hit me in the head like a hammer.

"I'm still the same boy that you knew. What I was thinking was that Friday is Karaoke night at the hotel bar. You told me you sing, and if you remember correctly, I was in chorus in high school. So does it interest you, just to cap off the evening?" I really was in the middle of a fantasy. It sounded perfect and I told him so. Karaoke started at 8.

Josh ran up to his room to put his presents away. I used the time to call Jon and briefly tell him about Tina, and running into Josh.

The waiter came with the drinks and the song list, which was extensive.

There were more people there our age and older than young people who probably were out at local bars and restaurants. It was very early for them.

That suited us fine. No one would make fun of our song choices.

I chose "Old Cape Cod" a song from the 50's that I always loved.

Josh thought he could have some fun with "Copacabana" and he was terrific. I wished this evening would never end.

We then decided to end the evening with a duet.

I was very into Rod Stewart's new series of "Great American Songbook" albums. One of my favorite songs, "For All We Know" seemed to fit right in with this whole experience. It is a very old song, recorded many times, but I got to know it from Rod's album. I asked Josh if he knew it. He said he had heard it before, and he would give it a try.

What he didn't know he would leave to me.

I started the song and he sang the next line. It wasn't perfect, but it conveyed the message: We did not know when or if we would see each other again.

Both of our eyes were moist when we finished.

It was 9:30 and time for me to go. I still had an hour's drive home.

I gathered my stuff and we walked into the lobby.

"That's not the way it's gonna go," he said earnestly.

"I am in New York a couple of times a year, and we will keep in touch and see each other again." We had exchanged phone numbers and emails at dinner.

"OK, then I have one last song for you to hear."

I opened my phone to the music app and handed it to him to listen to when we got outside. The song was "We Never Really Say Goodbye" by Captain and Tennille. It was the song we used on the last day of camp every year when I was a counselor. He listened and smiled.

"This is more like it," he said as he handed me back the phone.

He walked me to the garage and while we were waiting for my car he gave me one of his famous hugs, and then a kiss goodbye. The kiss lasted just a touch longer than a quick goodbye kiss. "Drive safely, and text me when you get home," he ordered.

"Have a good flight," I countered, "and I hope everything works out at home." "It will," he sighed.

The car came, he waved and he was gone.

The bubble burst.

I drove home listening to the news, and music and tried to keep my eyes on the road. Fortunately there was not a lot of traffic and I was home in less than an hour. And now I am seeing the visions on the ceiling. A vision slid into view.

A review of the wonderful day two old friends had in New York.

headlines

By Dennis Hawkins

There was a time when tabloids
mattered more many years ago,
then the poetry in headlines was clear
Headless Body in Topless Bar
the prose beneath - not so concise.
 Dirty Dozen: Crooked Cops Cracked
In Brooklyn's criminal court - charged
with a barrage of crimes from selling drugs
to stealing garbage cans from the 77th Precinct –
a putrid smell.
 First Fun, then Deadly Run
When white boys party in Howard Beach
ignite a bloody fight   racist attack
forcing a black youth to his death
on the Belt Parkway – hit by a passing car
his head cracked.
 Sliced and Diced
Describes a pickup in a bar
the attack in a Brooklyn garage,
the body tucked in the victim's
Crown Vic trunk, driven to Kentucky
to dispose of body parts – never found.
 Fractured Family: Columbo Chaos

Bodies drop like flies – mobsters
one innocent dies, law enforcers try
to stem the tide of mob homicides
to no avail, the DA subpoenas –
they all lie.
If it bleeds, it leads "The Wood" reads:
Happy Death Day
He wasn't expecting it
a drive-by on his birthday,
but in his 'hood
sometimes that's the surprise
before you die.

grandpa abe

By Steve Borodkin

Grandpa Abe, *my dad's father. Dressed in a white shirt open at the neck, suspenders, and brown slacks. Always with a pipe, notepad, and pencil. Writing something down in his ever-present notebook. Never looking up until I said, "Hey grandpa." This man became an unconditional counterweight to the darkness and depravity I experienced at home all of the time.*

Stage Left

Friday night, January 17th, 1964... I am nine years old. The opening performance of *Hello Dolly*. I remember it being ridiculously cold and snowing like mad. I was wearing my rubber galoshes (boots) over my shoes with the pant legs of my suit tucked into the tops. As a young kid, unnoticed, I always got to wander around the theaters I went to with Grandpa. The union would call him if one of the Broadway show orchestras needed a cellist. Grandpa Abe got to play his cello in the orchestra of a lot of Broadway shows through the 1960s. I went with him to quite a few. Always seeking out the stagehands and actors. Invariably, drawn to the side of the stage where I could just see the audience up front from behind the curtains. And be as close to the production on stage as I could without getting in the way. There I could feel the glorious, choreographed, stampeding energy of the live performance.

Not sure of the location or who took the photo. Looks like the late 1950s, early '60s. Abraham Borodkin was a poet, lyricist, artist, composer, master of four languages and self-expression and my buddy. Grandpa Abe, with his ever-present pipe. His spirit runs deep in my bones.

"What a sweet little boy! What is your name?"
"Stevie, my grandpa plays in the orchestra."
I stammered, "He, he plays the cello."
Staring down and smiling, she answered sweetly, "Well you stay right there, Stevie whose grandpa plays the cello, I'll sing this next song for you."

I was immediately enthralled by that amazingly infectious smile and the touch of Carol Channing's hands on my cheeks. I had no idea who she was, but she was bright and shiny, and larger than life.

I had been to Broadway performances before to hear my grandfather play, but this was my first opening night. The theater was packed. I stood there feeling that familiar magic starting to take hold, the anticipation of the live music beginning to course through my veins as the conductor raised his baton and the orchestra went silent, holding their breath, waiting for the conductor's command. For that brief moment, collectively, instinctively, the audience holds its breath as well. Then release, feeling the sound instantly flood the theater. Feeling the rumble in my stomach from the dozens of instruments as I watch the lights go up on stage.

The depth of Mrs. Channing's voice reached in and touched my heart, just as the palm of her hand had reached down and touched my cheek moments before.

I was able to experience *Hello Dolly* four times, standing stage left for every performance. Mrs. Channing said "hello" to me each night I showed up, even if it was a casual glance or a wink. The union called Grandpa Abe to another production two months later. She shook Grandpa's hand and thanked him for his contribution to the show before we left the theater for the final time.

Each one of Broadway's elaborate and extreme details gave me an undeniable feeling of freedom and energy. When I knew I was going to a weekend matinee, it didn't matter what performance it was. Who cared? I was dressed and good to go, standing by my grandfather's cello, packed in its case in his living room, thirty-minutes too early. Like a drug, I felt myself craving the sound, lights, and the unfiltered power of The Great White Way. I have no desire to participate in it, but instead, stand close enough as an observer to not miss one beat of its glorious heart.

Grandpa Abe introduced me to the conductor and all his friends in the orchestra each time we got to a new theater. We always got to walk through the side door with all the actors and other musicians. Some shows I was able to sit in the orchestra pit under the stage. Not being able to see the production at all. Even better, I got to watch the conductor elegantly guide my grandfather and his fellow musicians as they focused and swayed in time to the strokes of the conductor's baton. It was hypnotizing. A magical experience, hearing the singing and lyrics from above my head, and the profound musical accompaniment that danced all around me.

Abraham Borodkin, a Jewish Russian immigrant, who fled his homeland with my grandmother as young children, escaping the pogroms. Smuggled out of their villages on a potato cart, buried under sacks of potatoes, through dark cemeteries in the middle of the night to the shipping docks, to ships waiting to take them away from the terror of anti-Semitism for a price as they made their way with their families to Europe then to America, through Ellis Island.

Abraham was an intellect. He spoke fluently in three different languages. A consummate musician, composer, and painter, his eclectic library of musical compositions is a mix of jazz, chamber music, orchestral, and opera pieces. He was an ace at close to one hundred instruments. Through the 1950s, '60s, and '70s, a sizable amount of his work was performed regularly by other orchestras and bands for the *NBC Radio Hour*. He collaborated with Perry Como and Skitch Henderson & The Skitch Henderson Orchestra. He played at Carnegie Hall as well as the Lincoln Center. One of his greatest moments was playing on the first musical, live public radio broadcast on NPR in 1948, with the famous Springwood String Quartet. When my dad passed away back in 1998, I took all the boxes of my grandfather's work that my father had taken when his father died. I started to make my way through the vast treasure that made up the body of his work which included every composition he had, along with every handwritten notes and all the accompanying instrumentation. Some came with the matching vinyl recording. I came upon an urban-cool recording with all his original notation for each of the twenty-five instruments. A jazzy homage, big band piece, written in the early 1940's. It is a soundful, joy-filled proclamation of his love for New York City's vibrancy and the music of that time. Dedicated to, *"My friend, George Gershwin."*

"Grandpa Abe" is also published by Red Penguin Books in *Street Level* by Steve Borodkin.

the king and the lower east side

By Steve Borodkin

Summer, 1968

  The Lower East Side of Manhattan back in the late 1960s at its lowest level was divided into kingdoms. The stoops of the tenement buildings its thrones. The higher up you sat on the scarred and trampled stoop of your building, in some ways, the more of a made-man you were. You were a king. You received all kinds of cool shit. Free cigarettes and weed. If you were lucky enough to have a working girl on your turf, you got free pussy if you were old enough to care. As king, you could also get a bit off the top from whatever went down on your turf. That was, if you knew about it. There were so many people making so many deals and running so many frauds, it was hard to keep track most times. Somehow, we all got along.

  Two things on the street were never tolerated. It either got you hurt or dead. You did business in your space and, without exception, *never* spoke against or about anyone that you did business with. If you stayed cool, you could really get over without getting in each other's way. If you were lucky enough, you ended up with enough dough to treat yourself to a small bag of primo weed and a plate of matzo brie with a cup of hot chocolate at Ratner's, a huge dairy restaurant that served the best breakfast below Saint Marks Place. It was located on Delancey Street at the foot of the Williamsburg Bridge on the westbound side.

How did you get to be a king? I had no idea and really did not give a flying fuck. I had much bigger issues to contend with as a fourteen-year-old runaway. Being the king and getting free pussy and weed was the furthest thing from my mind. At the present time, not being part of any group and being the new kid on the block, and for a very brief time fresh meat, I was at the bottom of the food chain. Street level for now was off limits if I wanted to stay physically intact and keep whatever cash I had. To my way of thinking, the only way around this world of bullshit every day was cutting across the tenement rooftops five stories above the ground. I was tired of sneaking around my own neighborhood and even more tired of paying to get my ass kicked. I loved the idea of cutting out whole blocks of bullshit just by staying aloft. Jumping from building to building thrilled me. I fell in love with it. The freedom of cheating death rocked me to my core.

The stench of shit and garbage was too heavy to make it that high off the cement and asphalt below. Hundreds of feet above it all, the air was cleaner. Free to breathe. As I passed over each building, there were large pigeon coops housing dozens of well-fed birds. The cooing and muffled sound of their voices a soundtrack to my weightlessness. The men and boys who tended these coops would collect, feed, and train these birds. Releasing them, letting the flock circle overhead, leading them from the roof tops with long thin rods that they circled over their heads. Orchestrating the flock skillfully, and with a bit of luck, drawing pigeons from competing flocks from other rooftops to their own, lured by the alpha males. It was a peaceful and unencumbered world. Apart from the minutia and war zone below. These pigeons had names, like Bomber, Grey Baby, Blue Bell, Fly Boy, and Night Sky. The men who tended the birds would stop and watch me jump in calculated strides, bursting from one building to the next, flying, mocking their birds, landing feet first most times on the next building. I fell in love with the freedom of flight. As if I was Icarus. Reckless and defiant of all limitations, holding myself aloft through the two feet of air between each building. They'd wave to me with those *what the fuck* looks in their eyes. Sometimes I would stop, out of breath and bravery, peering over the side. My halted breath an acknowledgement of my immigrant status in this urban, alien, landscape. Staring down on streets teeming with life below, I sometimes thought when I finally do slip and fall, plummeting head first onto the pavement, I would be just another lost soul. Dead and pushed aside. My corpse left orphaned in the absence of my spirit as it slips away into the crowded, derelict humanity of my new neighborhood. I slipped one day as I launched myself through the air, just making it to the next building. Sitting on the opposite roof, cuts on my hands from a hard landing, with small pieces of broken bottles and dirt now embedded in the palms of my hand, my back up against the very wall I almost missed. Shaking, bleeding, I peed my pants. Coming to the realization that I *would* die from this subconscious, suicidal propensity. So, it seemed, like everyone else, the only way to get any approbation on the streets was to be a part of the machine that was the streets. I surmised that I was either going to be grease or gear. I chose gear. It was either that or go back to that fucking animal . . . my mother.

I sat there thinking about the repeated rapes and beatings that I had endured at her hands before I finally ran away. The unbearable shame of all of it coursed through my body; I was septic with the idea of pain as a tool, and I was done running. I had left home to save myself, not kill myself jumping tenement roofs. My anger of not wanting to be fucked over or touched anymore finally had fermented into a beautifully physical manifestation. Then something inside spoke to me; it kept repeating in my mind, blocking any other thoughts from penetrating. It said, *Fuck them all, Stevie, fuck them all to hell.* I listened intently. The stench of my own piss drying in my pants, the pain in my palms starting to throb was intoxicating. I fuckin' loved it. Violent retribution was on the menu and was best served cold.

"The King and the Lower East Side" is also published by Red Penguin Books in *Street Level* by Steve Borodkin.

the rats of new york city

by Laura Shenton

Whilst most New Yorkers pride themselves on their resilience, none can hold a candle to the city's true survivors: the magnificent rats of the Big Apple. These whiskered warriors, some approaching the size of small cats (or so the wide-eyed tourists claim), have turned the concrete jungle into their personal playground with characteristic American ambition.

In the finest tradition of New York City hustlers, these resourceful rodents have mastered the art of the five-borough feast. From the finest pizzerias in Manhattan, where they've been spotted dragging entire slices down subway stairs with remarkable panache, to the poshest bins of the Upper East Side, they display a culinary sophistication that would put many food critics to shame.

These enterprising creatures have adapted to city life with remarkable flair, developing what scientists suggest might be distinct regional accents in their squeaks – though whether they've mastered the distinctive "fuhgeddaboudit" remains a matter of scholarly debate. They've even mastered the art of urban navigation, scampering through the subway system with greater efficiency than most tourists armed with Google Maps.

Truth be told, these bedraggled beauties have become such an integral part of New York's character that they might as well feature on the city's coat of arms. After all, what better mascot for a city that never sleeps than a creature that's mastered the art of thriving in chaos, finding opportunity in every corner, and treating the city's obstacles as mere suggestions?

Indeed, in true New York fashion, these rats don't just survive – they flourish with a certain swagger that seems to say, "I'm walking here!" Though perhaps "scurrying" would be more precise.

the bobblehead

by William John Rostron

What is the typical New Yorker like? With the variations of race, religion, and ethnicity, it would take a lot of work to answer that question. However, ask me that same question about the typical New York *Sports* fan, and I will claim complete expertise...and then tell you the story of "The Bobblehead."

How Big Apple fans "root, root for the home team" is unique—no matter which home team it is. Additionally, that rooting can be positive...or negative. After all, they don't call it the "Bronx Cheer" for nothing! New Yorkers always become emotionally involved with their favorites—sometimes too much. That is perhaps my one qualm about New York fans—the habit of a fan claiming pseudo-ownership of a team. "*We* won last night." "Boy, that play *we* made last night." I'm sorry, you never donned the uniform...*you* didn't win the game. *You* didn't hit the home run or catch the fly ball. The team you root for did all that, and you can rejoice in it; however, you cannot claim ownership. Sorry for the slight diversion before getting on with the story of "The Bobblehead."

I am an enthusiastic, obsessive New York fan. So, of course, the next logical question would be, "Which team?" My response is unequivocal, "All of them." If you put a "NY" on your hat, helmet, or shirt, I am your fan for life. Do you see a problem here? If not, you don't follow sports too closely. This interesting dilemma only exists in New York, Chicago, and Los Angeles, not coincidentally, the three largest cities in the United States. In baseball, each city has two teams. A common belief is that if you are a fan of one, you must hate the other. Sometimes, these disagreements result in physical confrontations. I once witnessed an all-out brawl at the Mets-Yankees game. I was so amused as I sat with my mixed group of Yankee and Met fans that I cannot remember who won the fight...or the game. Still working my long-winded way to the story of "The Bobblehead."

I am a fan of both the Yankees and the Mets. I am told this is a delusional fantasy. Yet, my reasoning is solid. I was too young to remember when the traitorous Dodgers and Giants were local teams and so had none of the hatred for the Yankees instilled in me as a youth by an older generation of those fans for those teams. Simply put, the Yankees were the only team in town when I discovered the wonderful game of baseball. Of course, it didn't hurt that they seemed to be winners every year—a kid's dream.

Then the Mets were created in 1962. They were a Queens team, the county where I resided, and it seemed natural to become their fan. However, my Yankee-hating (ex-Dodger and Giant fans) told me it was impossible. I asked why. These two teams would never compete against each other because they were in different leagues. The only place that could happen would be in the World Series, and there was no chance of that happening soon. In their first year, the Mets set a record for losses (120) in a season—a feat that has not been duplicated in sixty years.

Eventually, baseball started interleague play, and I had a problem. How do you watch a game where you don't want either team to lose? Matters got even worse when the two teams met in the 2000 World Series. Not only did it require a split allegiance, but it also almost led to divorce court. My wife is as much a baseball fan as I am. However, whereas I *lean* toward the Yankees, she *favors* the Mets. So for the first time in the thirty-eight years of the Mets' existence, there was taunting and teasing within the Rostron household. I will try to avoid mentioning that the Yankees won that series four games to one. (I wrote that I would *try* not to mention it; I didn't say that I actually wouldn't mention it.)

This love of baseball by both my wife and I caused us to set out in retirement to see every baseball stadium in America. We couldn't always see one of our home teams on these tours, but sometimes we did. We had just seen the Mets play in Philadelphia when we drove our RV to Cleveland to see an Indians – Twins game. While at that game, we looked at the scoreboard and noticed that the Mets were playing the final game of their series in Milwaukee. We packed up the RV at midnight and headed to Wisconsin, hoping to arrive in time for the game. And that is where the tale of "The Bobblehead" begins.

After driving through the night and parking our RV in a campground, we barely had time to drive to the stadium in the SUV that we towed along with us. Imagine our surprise when we reached the ticket booth and they explained that the game was sold out! How could that be? The Brewers were not in a pennant race. They were not a good team and had not sold out any other game that year. After we got entry with standing-room-only seats, we discovered a bizarre reason for the packed house—it was "Derrick Turnbow Bobblehead Night." So what? Have you never heard of him? You are not alone. I have told this story to numerous devout baseball fans in the past twenty years, who have all displayed ignorance of this little-known relief pitcher. His claim to fame was that he had recorded saves in the first four games of that season—a feat never before or after achieved. This accomplishment meant a great deal to Milwaukee fans. Go figure.

We settled in to watch the game and enjoyed mingling with the local fans. This was one of the reasons that we enjoyed our tour of the stadiums. Besides baseball, we were interested in the food and beverage choices, the architecture of the stadium, and, most of all, the people. We found that standing increased our enjoyment and understanding of the Brewer crowd. They were friendly and welcoming to "the strangers from New York." We talked to many of them while the game proceeded. The Brewers were leading for most of the game, 3–0.

"So, what do you think?" One of our new friends asked.

I didn't know if he was referring to the actual architecture of Miller Field, which had a spectacular retractable dome, or to the general experience of a game in Milwaukee. So I gave a very noncommital "very nice." One of the other guys was more specific.

"So, how does this compare to a game in New York?"

Again I didn't want to seem obnoxious. However, my wife intervened and said, "It's different." You could hear the sound of a can of worms opening up.

"Different, how?" Can of worms alert.

"Just different, that's all," she said, but I knew that wasn't going to float. So it was time to pull the bandage off all at once.

"Okay, in New York, we yell all the time. We yell encouragement when we are losing and jeer at the opponent when we are winning."

"But we cheer, don't we?"

"You cheer when something happens. In New York, we cheer *to make it* happen. And we don't just cheer, we boo…a lot. And it is not always at the other team. So if you are a New York player and you are not performing as well as the fans expect, you will hear sustained chanting. Strike out in a key situation, and you won't be able to hear yourself think."

"That doesn't sound nice."

"Nothing is nice about us if you don't perform as well as we expect. Maybe it pushes them harder or keeps the weak at heart from ever coming to our town. Whatever it is, it creates great sports moments and winning teams."

"So all you care about is winning?"

"Is there anything else? But seriously, even if we lose, we have a great time—one you can never forget."

"I still don't get it."

While all this conversation was going on, the Mets had narrowed the gap to 3-2. I saw the worry on their faces. Then, suddenly, that fear, that desperation, turned to elation. Derrick Turnbow was coming in the top of the ninth to save the game. Derrick Turnbow of the immortal bobblehead that every ticketholder received upon entering the stadium that day. Derrick Turnbow, holder of the four straight saves at the opening of the season record. He would shut off the Mets and preserve the game for the adoring home fans.

Except he didn't. Paul LoDuca, the Mets catcher, hit a two-run homer on his first pitch. This put the Mets ahead on their way to an eventual 4 – 3 visiting team victory.

"That's too bad," was the general attitude of our newly made friends. A resignation to defeat without any recourse seemed inevitable to them. But, oh well, tomorrow's another day.

It was a perfect teaching moment.

"No, you can't be just disappointed that your team lost. You have to be angry... and let someone know it...loudly."

"We don't understand."

I looked at the Derrick Turnbow bobbleheads that each of us held.

"If this was New York and Derrick Turnbow had given up the winning home run on his bobblehead night, there would have been swift and fitting retribution for that one act of failure. There would have been consequences."

"Like what?"

"So, how many Brewer fans were here today?"

"About 33,000."

"In New York, 33,000 thousand people would have opened those boxes holding the bobbleheads...33,000 would have taken out their bobbleheads... 33,000 would have ripped the heads off, and 33,000 would have thrown them out onto the field."

"Are you kidding? These are valuable collector items. They will be worth big money."

I didn't know then what they considered big money, but my point was falling on deaf ears. Finally, I saw a passing man wearing a hat with a New York logo and called out to him.

"Hey, Fella, if a player gave up the winning home run on his bobblehead night, what would we do in New York?"

I could not have gotten a more timely response if he had been a shill that I planted in the audience. He pantomimed taking the figure out of the box, tearing its head off, and then throwing it like a hand grenade. He laughed and continued on his way to the exit. Do I know my New York sports fans or what?

I smiled and bid farewell to the very nice people we had spent a wonderful day with. (Not just because the Mets won.) I know in my heart that I had used the bobblehead analogy to honestly explain what a New York sports fan was like. Still, I don't think they got it.

However, our friends were right about one thing. My wife and I sold our Derrick Turnbow collectible bobbleheads on eBay for $50 each two weeks later. The bidding all came from the Milwaukee area. It was perfect timing. They became worthless less than a year later when Turnbow was gone from major league baseball.

in the heights: another side of new york city

by William John Rostron

Broadway! Skyscrapers! Central Park! Wall Street! This is the New York City that the world envisions. In reality, that is only Manhattan, merely one-fifth of a quintet of boroughs that make up the famed metropolis. I can't say that the outsiders' description is completely wrong. I was officially born and raised within the political entity of New York City. However, being in one of the "outer boroughs" caused us to develop a definite inferiority complex. Still, when we traveled on the F train into Manhattan from Queens, we told everyone we were "going to the city." I lived in one of the other hamlets in the municipality—one so small that much of the population of the largest city in America had never heard of it.

    The town of Cambria Heights first came into being in the late 1920s. Up until that time, the area had been mostly farmland. Its name had been derived from the Cambria Construction Company of Pennsylvania, which had been instrumental in constructing buildings in the area. The "Heights" designation was laughable to most people who had traveled almost anywhere outside the city. Cambria challenged the illustrious "mountain" villages of Jackson Heights and Richmond Hill for the honor of being the *highest* point in the county of Queens, with an oxygen-threatening elevation of 49 feet above sea level.

From the beginning, the area had been populated almost exclusively by Irish, Italian, German, and Jewish families who could not afford to live in the more established neighborhoods of Brooklyn or Queens or the affluent suburbs of adjoining Nassau County. Being at the extreme outer fringes of New York City, it received services only after most of the city's budget had been spent on the upscale sections of Manhattan. When there was a power failure, it might get fixed in the Heights...eventually. When a water main broke, it might get repaired...eventually. Moreover, if there was a heavy snowstorm, it was only hoped that the city plows would somehow locate Linden Boulevard sometime before the spring thaw.

People had lived in the area for decades before the city of New York saw fit to extend gas lines to the hamlet. As a result, it was commonly referred to as "Kerosene Hill" well into the twentieth century. This condescending nickname referred to its only source of power until the advent of World War II.

The post-World War II period brought an influx of returning veterans who wanted homes to raise their baby boomer families. Unfortunately, their finances relegated them to this tiny corner of the city where resources and transportation were almost non-existent. They also witnessed the construction of the Cross Island Parkway on their eastern border. Besides offering most New Yorkers an excellent North-South thoroughfare, it also succeeded in permanently and irrevocably cutting off Cambria Heights from the wealthy and sprawling suburbs of neighboring Nassau County.

Yet, the area grew into a thriving community with its own identity. Its bustling economic and cultural life flourished around the main street of Linden Boulevard. With an overwhelming percentage of the residents being Roman Catholic, Sacred Heart Church and its extensive adult membership and Catholic school population generated many of the community's social activities. The adults attended church-sponsored dances and communion breakfasts. Some hot summer nights they sat outside on their "stoops" with the neighbors and jokingly "wondered what the poor people were doing." Though Mr. Softee and the Good Humor Man made their annual attempts at drumming up business, "Joe, The Ice Cream Man" owned Cambria Heights, and buying from anyone else was considered nothing short of mortal sin.

The CYO baseball team from Sacred Heart won the championship of all Brooklyn and Queens in 1963. This meant that the fourteen players were the best of all the teams created in an area of over three million people. This pinnacle of success fueled the already evident community spirit of the 1950s and early 1960s, creating an atmosphere that would never be forgotten. Finally, pride could be found on the streets of this tight-knit community. This lower-middle-class neighborhood had become a place no one would ever want to leave.

Yet, by 1970, over 90% of the white population of Cambria Heights had moved away. The six years of this mass exodus were a time of change throughout the city, indeed, throughout the country. However, it was nowhere more violent or explosive than in this tiny hamlet. An astute real estate investor might have seen the neighborhood's downfall coming and sold early in 1964 when the prices were highest. This area was "pretty" but poor by the standards of its surrounding neighborhoods of Queens Village and Laurelton. Its residents did not have much material wealth. Though they worked hard, they frequently held jobs at the lowest pay levels in a city. There were so many social and economic layers above them that they strained their necks looking up.

However, they did have their homes, and they did have their neighborhood. Right or wrong, their source of pride often revolved around their turf being exclusively white. Later years would judge these people harshly in terms of their racist beliefs; however, the decade of the 1960s was a different time. People in poor white areas knew almost nothing about those different from them. The late-twentieth-century concept of diversity had not yet made it into this community. Socializing or even speaking to anyone "too different" was almost non-existent, and most people rarely married outside their nationality or religion. A "mixed marriage" usually meant that someone of Irish ethnicity had somehow found common ground with an equally open-minded Italian. The world in Manhattan may have moved way beyond this kind of thinking, but the outer boroughs remained steeped in the past. Sociologists have speculated that this misplaced pride in poor white areas resulted from the residents' feelings that there was at least some group even lower on the food chain than them. In their eyes, a white ghetto was considered a step above a black ghetto.

These feelings were incited and amplified by real estate agents looking to make exorbitant commissions on the buying and selling of the houses in Cambria Heights. Residents were constantly bombarded with the idea that once their neighborhood became integrated, the value of their only material object of value, their house, would be gone. Their lives would become hell on Earth. Interestingly, most of these agents did not have an address with the newly invented zip code designation 11411.

In 1964, just as the Beatles were triumphantly conquering the hearts of American teens, Cambria Heights was poised for the dissolution of its existing way of life. Located between the overwhelming black neighborhoods of Hollis, St. Albans, and Jamaica and the solid brick wall of the costly areas of Nassau County, the residents developed a siege mentality. Pressed from all sides, they found themselves with very few options. It would take one loose brick, and their fortress would crumble.

Officially, it was just a road called Springfield Boulevard. However, no one on either side of the two-lane blacktop road did not know that it was "the line." With a few rare exceptions, everyone west of the line was black, and everyone east was white. Of course, there were genuine racists on both sides of the line.

However, what made this time different was how many people felt nothing but fear: fear of violence, fear of change, fear of property value decline, and fear of the unknown. Therefore, blacks and whites kept to themselves, without ever venturing to the other side of the line except at their own risk. That was until the change.

The schoolyard surrounding P.S. 147 was tucked neatly into the neighborhood only three blocks from "The Line." It was the center of white teenage social life in the Heights. Whether it was stickball, handball, softball, or goofballs, it was going on there. The very young, with their innocent athletic pursuits, mingled unnoticed with gang-related and vastly horny mid-teens and the burnt-out, strung-out late teens. It was all happening at the yard.

In its infinite wisdom, the City of New York had finally decided to spend some of its tax dollars to redo the schoolyard of P.S. 147. New blacktop, new softball fields, and the construction of basketball courts were an effort to improve the lives of the area's young people. Unfortunately, the politician who came up with this pork-barrel legislation had either never been to the site or was highly misguided in his integration attempts. Blue-collar white kids generally did not play basketball in the Heights. They had no practical use for these new courts. In fact, they resented the loss of space from the handball and stickball courts sacrificed for these unwanted hoops. Yet, their reasoning paled compared to what they viewed as the other undesirable result of the changes.

The beautiful, newly constructed courts served only as a beacon of temptation for "the line" to be obliterated by the influx of young boys of color from the other side. It would not be long before the invisible barrier of Springfield Boulevard was breached, and the conflict began. Indoctrinated by the pressure tactics of the realtors, many white adults reacted to integration by putting their houses up for sale. However, the young hormone-engorged white males viewed this challenge to their turf as a call to arms. Unaware that their parents were in the process of pulling up stakes and heading for the white suburbs of Long Island, they prepared to fight to the death against the encroachment of "outsiders."

And this is where I enter the story. I was fourteen in 1963 and lived just one block east of "the line," thus giving me a front-row seat to most of the violence. Like most young males in Cambria, I knew how to fight and therefore was heavily recruited by the local gangs for service on the front line. I would say I went AWOL, except I never enlisted. I never became a part of the violence by choice. I didn't believe in the cause because of three factors: Earl, Mary, and the Yardbirds.

Following a path many in my area took, I spent my high school years in a Catholic High School. I also spent those same years commuting by bus and train to get there. A young man got on the same bus as me every day—only *west of the line*. His name was Earl, and we not only went to the same school but were in homeroom together for four years. He was one of the nicest guys I have ever met. How could I justify the violence and hatred many of my friends proposed based on race? If this one person could be so good, this dispelled any racist argument of inherent evil. Earl was an example of what every boy or man, white or black, should strive to be—perhaps more than he needed to be.

We all had to wear jackets and ties to school every day. However, it didn't take me long to realize that Earl's shirts were starched, and his jacket and pants were always newly pressed. So I asked him about it as a friend, and he gave me a quizzical look that said, *you really should know the answer to that.*

"How many black guys are in our grade?"

"Two," I answered, embarrassed that this number was two out of 325.

He looked at me with a small smile and said, "You see what's happening in Cambria. You see what's going on in the world. My parents believe everything about us needs to be perfect to be equal. I'm not going to give anyone an excuse to look down at me."

"I don't think that way about you."

"Yeah, but you're just a little shithead." He laughed boisterously. As part of his "perfect" facade, he had never used even vaguely off-color language. This was his way of showing that he could let down his perfect guard to me because we were friends. I was honored. A few years ago I looked him in up in our alumni directory. Earl was a doctor at a preeminent medical facility.

Then there was Mary. To be specific, Mary Weiss.

Many a young man throughout America lusted for Mary Weiss, the lead singer of The Shangri-Las. Her long blonde hair and the pouty grimace that appeared on an album cover only increased the sales of these "girl group" phenoms. In an era of The Shirelles, The Supremes, and a thousand other groups singing about their devotions to the opposite sex, the Shangri-Las remained the musical version of the "Great White Hope." Not lost in this image was the fact that these girls sang about a life they knew about first-hand from growing up in Cambria Heights.

In the press releases that accompanied the group on tour, references were made that they came from "a rough section of Queens, New York." Unlike most images fabricated for the record-buying public, this statement was true. The people of Cambria Heights knew how rough it was in their area, and they had watched and listened to these hometown stars sing about a life they shared in common with the group.

Before stardom, the girls had hung out at Ed's Luncheonette on Linden Boulevard, and the words to their songs were very autobiographical. Though the real "Leader of the Pack" did not die as in the song, "Jimmy" was one of their boyfriends. Yet, even as the Shangri-Las were singing about gang life in Southeast Queens, the scenery rapidly changed to something they would not even recognize when they returned from touring. Their life had been a story of white-on-white violence reminiscent of a fifties scenario that was rapidly fading away. The stories they sang about had been fights between the guys who frequented Ed's and their rivals, Renos. Their battles had been legendary in the eyes of all the young white boys growing up in the area. But the Renos' and Ed's gangs no longer existed. They had gone extinct in a changing world. Their members had gone on to jobs, families, and life. They had grown up. This had left a void in the gang arena. There was no one left to "defend the border."

A new type of gang in the Heights rose from the ashes of these two groups. Gone was the "hanging out" in a dinette replete with milkshakes and girls. Gone was any social aspect of the memberships. This group would have its origins in the schoolyards and basements throughout the entire neighborhood. It would include those who attended the local public school and any of the area's Catholic high schools. It would not be exclusive but rather inclusive of any guy who wanted to "defend" their home and neighborhood from its imminent destruction. It dwarfed all other fledgling groups.

Yet, not everyone thought of the Shangri-Las in terms of the gang lifestyle. A small group of Cambria teens emulated another side of their story. They saw a group of kids who had made it out of the neighborhood and had done it through music. Mary and the rest of the Shangri-Las became the people I wanted to model the direction of my life after. I wanted to escape the violence with music.

I rebuffed all offers of gang membership, choosing privately and publicly to use the excuse that I had no time because of the band. My band progressed and is a story to be told at another time. However, music, specifically the song lyrics, always crowded my brain and influenced my thought process.

One song specifically spoke to the issues of the time and helped me clarify where I stood. "Better Man Than I" by the Yardbirds had a refrain that repeatedly stated that you were a "better man than I" if you could believe certain concepts." Like "Can you tell a wise man by the way he speaks or spells? Is this more important than the stories that he tells?" And then the line that put everything in perspective to my fifteen-year-old mind.

Can you condemn a man,
If your faith he doesn't hold?
Say the color of his skin,
Is the color of his soul?

. . .

After college in 1972, I moved sixty miles from Cambria Heights to take a teaching job on Long Island. Occasionally, if I am passing by, I drive through the area of my youth. The neighborhood is neat and nicely kept up. Populated mainly by West Indian and other black families, it is considered one of the better areas of New York—not the "hell" predicted. I often wonder what would have happened if the white residents had not been scared off by the rumors promulgated by the blockbusting real estate agents. Was it real racism at play, or simply ignorance? If things had gone differently, could this area have been the shining example of integration that the nation so yearned for? I guess we'll never know.

Though I often think about those days, my life moved on. Then, a few years ago, an ex-student contacted me and said he would like to meet with me. I had been his sixth-grade trade teacher a quarter of a century before, and he wanted to talk to me about the good old days when I let him play guitar during recess in my class. He had been one of the few black kids in our school, and he had dealt with it well, becoming extremely popular. He is now a famous musician who can be seen nightly on a late-night show playing with the same enthusiasm I saw in that twelve-year-old.

He came out to my house, located 60 miles east of New York City, and we talked long into one Sunday night. He took out his guitar and played for me, and I was duly impressed with how far he had come since he had exhibited raw but untrained talent so long ago.

As he went to leave that night to go home to his wife and kids in Brooklyn, I asked him how he had happened to be on Long Island. Though raised in Holbrook, NY, Kirk now spends most of his time on tours or playing nightly with The Roots on the Tonight Show. He replied that he had just returned from taking his mother to a family function in Queens, where most of his relatives lived. I asked him where in Queens he had been? His reply was simple.

"Oh, it's a place you probably never heard of . . . Cambria Heights."

An online article in April 2025 cited Cambria Heights as one of the five best Black neighborhoods in America.

the big walk

Michael P. Kusen

We lived in Maspeth in Queens, which is part of New York City. Maspeth is named for a tribe of Indians who originally lived there. We lived up on the plateau in Maspeth, me, Carl and Jack with a bunch of other kids on Sixty-fourth Street. At the very top of our block, where it leveled off, you could look towards the west and see the Empire State Building in the Manhattan skyline. Maspeth was a great place to grow up in when we were kids in the 1950's – it had lots of vacant lots with trees and bushes that were miniature forests where we played games as pirates, cowboys, Indians, Robin Hood or Peter Pan and we built huts out of branches with thick leaves that we wove together. But this story isn't about playing in the lots or the other kids on the block – it's about one summer morning long ago when Jack and Carl and I decided to take a walk that turned into an adventure....

"My dad told me that Grand Avenue goes right down to the Williamsburg Bridge." I said looking up at Jack as we stood on the sidewalk across the street from his house.

"Yeah, so," Jack said.

"Well you wanna find out?"

"Find out what?"

"How long it takes to get there."

"To the bridge? Are you kidding?"

"No – it's straight down Grand Avenue – we can't get lost."

And that's how our adventure started. We began walking down the hill towards Grand Avenue. Halfway down the hill Carl spotted us from across the road as he was coming out of his driveway. He called out, "Hey you guys, wait up – where're you going?" Jack and I looked at each other and we both smirked knowing that we didn't want to tell Carl where we were headed. Sometimes you can do that with someone that you know really well – you can just look at each other and know what your pal is thinking.

"We're going to Grand Avenue," Jack said.

"For what?" Carl said as he crossed the road and came up to us.

"For a walk to see what's doin' on the avenue," I said.

So the three of us, Carl at eleven, Jack at twelve and me at ten years of age set off towards Grand Avenue. When we got to Grand Avenue we made a right turn and continued walking along on the sidewalk as we browsed in the store windows. As we strolled along Carl asked us where we were headed and why didn't we go another way. But Jack and I just kept our little secret and talked about other things as we walked along. After a while we had left the shopping section of Grand Avenue and were walking past residential homes as we kept walking towards the factory area. "Why are you guys going this way?" Carl blurted out. "There's nothing down there."

But we just kept walking along, occasionally picking up a bottle cap here and there or a bent twig as a walking stick and lightly whipped each other as we grabbed it from one another. We walked passed the tall factory lofts on the lower end of Grand Avenue and under the railroad trestle at Rust Street. Rust Street was named because it was originally built on discarded rusty old iron rails from the nearby railroad that ran through the factory area. Carl was getting more and more anxious about where we were going as we approached the Penny Bridge. The Penny Bridge was a short narrow bridge that goes over a tributary of Newtown Creek – years ago you had to pay a penny toll to cross it – it was also part of the irregular Brooklyn/Queens borderline.

"I'm not going any further," Carl protested. "I'm not going over that bridge – that's Brooklyn."

We stopped and stared at each other for a moment, then Jack looked at me and nodded his head.

"Ok – you want to know where we're going?" I said.

"Yeah, that would be nice."

"To the Williamsburg Bridge."

Jack shrugged and smiled watching Carl get excited.

"Are you crazy? Are you both crazy?"

"No," I countered, "It's straight ahead – straight down there." I pointed towards the Penny Bridge.

"You shoulda told me. You shoulda told me from the start."

"Well then maybe you wouldn't have come – maybe you would have just called us crazy and stayed on the block? But now you're here so what are you gonna do now – quit? Quit and go back home?

"You shoulda told me," Carl repeated. Jack stood there with his arms folded grinning like the Cheshire Cat.

"Well you gonna quit or are you gonna go with us to the Williamsburg Bridge?" I said.

"I don't quit, I'm not a quitter – if you can do it so can I," Carl protested.

And with that the three of us, like *The Three Musketeers*, continued on our adventure as we walked towards the Penny Bridge. "I don't quit," Carl said one more time to make sure that we knew he was not a quitter, "But you're still crazy – both of you are crazy – and you shoulda told me."

After crossing the Penny Bridge, we passed through the factory area on the Brooklyn side and continued on as factory lofts slowly diminished and stores, restaurants, taverns and beauty parlors began to take their place. We were in Greenpoint,

Brooklyn making our way towards Williamsburg and the famed Williamsburg Bridge. As we walked weaving and browsing we occasionally looked up for reassurance to see GRAND ST boldly printed on corner street signs. We hadn't noticed the subtle way that Grand Avenue becomes Grand Street when we passed over the Penny Bridge exiting Queens and entering Brooklyn. When we passed Bushwick Avenue, Jack began to read aloud the street signs: "Humboldt Avenue, Graham Avenue – hey look Manhattan Avenue – here in Brooklyn – how about that we're at Manhattan and Grand. And I feel grand, and life is grand." Jack began to giant step and skip-step along as we crossed the street. It didn't matter to us if it was Grand Avenue or Grand Street. We knew we were on a grand adventure – what mattered, all that mattered – was that everything was grand and the Williamsburg Bridge was straight ahead. We didn't know exactly where the line was between the neighborhoods of Greenpoint and Williamsburg. But somewhere as we paraded down the sidewalk and passed people and looked in store windows we passed from Greenpoint into Williamsburg and continued on – block after block until finally we reached a large open traffic plaza and across the distance of the plaza was the entrance to the Williamsburg Bridge.

"Wow," I said. There it was in front of us across the winding lanes of cars whizzing by. We had to get closer and at least touch the foundation to know that we really did it – that we were really here at the Williamsburg Bridge. So, we circled to the right along the sidewalk bordering the plaza. Until we finally were able to cross the traffic lanes and get right up to where the dark castle-like foundation stones of the great bridge touched the earth in Brooklyn. There we stood at the very foundation of the bridge and we rubbed our hands along the old stone blocks that made up the base support of the bridge. We walked along the foundation wall and then we saw a wide tunnel passageway in the foundation that was wide enough for cars but there were no cars. We walked into the passageway and in the center of this tunnel in the foundation there was a wide ramp leading up into the bridge.

Jack read the sign above the ramp, "Pedestrians Only."

"Pedestrians?" I said, "what's a pedestrian?"

Carl laughed, "We're pedestrians, you dope. Pedestrian means not driving in a car – people who walk on the sidewalk. And after walking here we are first-class pedestrians."

We stood there, the three of us, in a brief silence staring at the entrance and the wide paved path that stretched up going on and on seemingly forever into the heart of the bridge. The same thought started buzzing in each of our heads. We looked at each other. I bit down on my lip. Jack's eyes twinkled and he started to laugh. Carl threw open his arms and said, "No – no, I'm not going over the bridge." Jack spun on one heel as he continued laughing.

"We're here," I said, "it's the middle of the day – we got plenty of time – we gotta go over."

"I told you, you guys are crazy, no, no, enough, now. Let's go home."

"I can't – we can't, we can't quit now – think how great it must be up on the bridge and we can tell everybody that we walked to Manhattan – Manhattan, man – Manhattan!" Jack looked up toward the bridge and I knew he was thinking of the view up there and he wanted to see it.

I turned and got up close to Carl "Come on Carly, you're not gonna chicken out now, are ya?" I said.

"Don't start that crap? You know I'm not a quitter little man." Carl said as he got in my face. But the decision had already been made because as I backed up from Carl – we both turned to see Jack already a good way up the path into the bridge, running at a good clip. The challenge was on – who would be the first to the top of the bridge. Carl and I dashed up the path trying to catch up to Jack who had the longest legs and was sure to maintain his lead. Being smaller, I trailed Carl at first but he slowed down occasionally letting me catch up only to dash ahead again. I wasn't sure if he was teasing me or cared enough not to abandon me. But when we did run side by side he would look over at me and say, "You shoulda told me – you dachshund you – you and that giraffe."

Jack was up at the top of the path looking out over the East River at Manhattan when we finally caught up with him. My words sputtered out as I tried to catch my breath, "Wow – this is great!" I said looking out at the view. We spent the next few minutes running from side to side to take in all the vistas of Manhattan, Brooklyn, and distant Queens behind us.

Running down on the other side of the bridge was a breeze. We changed our pace from giant skips to trots and galloping leaps as we made our way to the bottom to set foot on Delancey Street in Manhattan. We had done it – we had walked into Manhattan – it was midday the sun was shining brightly and it felt like it was shining just for us.

Orchard Street was just a few blocks ahead and our adventure fever kicked in – we all wanted to go and walk up Orchard Street to see all the merchandise overflowing along the storefronts and sidewalk. We had all been to Orchard Street and it was just an exciting place to be – like a carnival. In a few minutes we were there walking north up Orchard Street, zigzagging on the sidewalk and gutter in and around the river of pants, socks, shoes, toys, bolts of material, knickknacks, on and on it went. We were like leaves floating on a winding stream being carried by some magical energy beneath our feet. In a few blocks we reached East Houston Street running east to west. It was the downtown borderline. All the streets behind us to the south were named streets. But once you crossed East Houston Street, there was First Street and Second Street and so on up to two hundred and something streets. To the right were the Avenues A, B, C, D and once you got past Fourteenth Street the named and numbered avenues kicked in to formalize the famous midtown Manhattan street grid. It was all too irresistible, East Houston Street stood like a giant defiant border challenging us – like the Rubicon to Caesar or the Rio Grande to John Wayne. We had to cross East Houston – we had to put our feet on the giant Manhattan grid that lay on the other side.

"First Street," Jack said pointing across East Huston Street. That was the next goal – we all knew it. There was no hesitation, not even from Carl. Now we were all crazy together. When the traffic light turned green we dashed off the curb kicking away the bottom of Manhattan as we sprinted across three lanes, skipped over the center meridian and crossed the north side three lanes to arrive at the corner intersection of First Street and First Avenue. We weren't just in Manhattan – we were in Manhattan proper. We plopped down on the curb and congratulated each other with quick flashes of what we had seen and heard on our great journey today. After a few minutes of resting on the curb we were undecided about exactly what to do – but we had a new sense of confidence.

We had come from Grand Avenue in Maspeth, Queens – crossed the Penny Bridge into Greenpoint, Brooklyn – crossed over the East River on the Williamsburg Bridge to land in Manhattan! We were basking in pride and now there were no barriers that we could not navigate. So, we figured that maybe we had a little more time left to explore Manhattan before we should turn around and start home. With our spirits emboldened we began to walk up First Avenue with as cavalier an attitude as any *Three Musketeers* could have.

It didn't take long for us to reach Fourteenth Street – we were at the top of our game with our adrenal pumps working overtime. "How about the Empire State Building?" I said. Both Jack and Carl stopped and stared at me. "You can see it from our block. Wouldn't it be great to get to it? Then we could point to it and tell everybody in Maspeth that we walked to it. Wouldn't that be great?"

"Oh, yeah great," Jack said, "How far is it?"

"Thirty-Sixth Street," Carl said, "I'm pretty sure – yeah it's Thirty-Sixth Street."

"That's about twenty blocks from here," Jack said, sliding his hands into his back pockets.

"Twenty-two blocks," Carl corrected.

"Twenty-two blocks, that's nothing," I said.

Jack took his hands out of his pockets and put his open right hand near my face, "We gotta go back ..." Carl looked around, stretching his neck but not saying anything.

I looked back and forth at my partner's faces trying to judge their moods, "But look how close we are – twenty blocks."

"Twenty-two," Carl corrected again.

"But think how great it would be to get to the Empire State Building. It would be great, really great." I said.

"Let's do it," Carl called out. "You two started this crazy thing but I'm in it now! – and I want to go to the Empire State Building before I quit."

Jack looked at the two of us with the eye of an older brother. "If we do the Empire State Building – that's it – if we get there it's turn-around-time – cause it's starting to get a little late, y'know."

"Let's go," Carl said, leading the way up First Avenue towards Fifteenth Street. "But you guys shoulda told me. You shoulda told me at the start."

When we reached Thirty-Sixth Street we looked at the canyons of buildings around us but there was no Empire State Building. Jack asked a passer-by and found out that we had to walk west to Fifth Avenue and then down to Thirty-fourth Street. Jack put his hand on Carl's shoulder and said, "It's not Thirty-sixth Street, it's Thirty-fourth Street and we have to go over to Fifth Avenue."

"Ok, ok, I was a little off – but close."

"Come on, let's get go'in," I said.

Off we went, *the Musketeers* were off again – walking west on Thirty-Sixth Street over to Fifth Avenue. A block away from the Empire State Building we stretched our necks looking up at it as we approached. Once inside we strolled around the lobby admiring the Art Deco designs, especially the elevator doors. We had no money to take the elevator up to the observation deck – but believe it or not – we didn't care, we were there on the ground floor and it was great just to be there. This was the final glory of our great adventure. And now it was time to go home. As we made our way through the revolving doors on Fifth Avenue a thought spun around in my brain – maybe we could go home by another route – a shorter route.

"Hey," I said as we hit the sidewalk. "What if we go home over the Fifty-ninth Street Bridge? Isn't that closer?"

"The Fifty-ninth Street Bridge?" Jack said, wondering.

Carl interjected, "Yeah, it's closer and it drops you on Queens Boulevard. We could take that straight up to Woodside and then over to Maspeth."

Jack didn't say a word for a minute but looked up north and then down south along Fifth Avenue. "All I know is it's get'in late… we got to make up our minds how to get home."

We bounced a few more ideas around and then headed east along Thirty-fourth Street planning to turn north on Second Avenue because we knew that would lead to the foot of the Fifty-ninth Street Bridge. About forty minutes later we were there and began hiking up the walking path of the Fifty-Ninth Street Bridge. We were a bit tired but still full of confidence – we couldn't wait to get home and tell everybody what we had done. We walked along chattering over each other's words and taking in the East River View as we neared the apex of the bridge. Then suddenly we were stunned to see that the walking path was blockaded with plywood and cement barriers and a sign that read "Do Not Enter Under Construction."

We were in the middle of this giant bridge spanning the East River and could go no further. We looked out onto the roadway where the cars were whizzing along. We all thought the same thing – it would be too dangerous to climb over the barriers and walk on the roadway. We had to go back and we needed a new plan. As we walked all the way back to our starting point in Manhattan we hassled each other about our predicament – blaming and accusing in gruff tones and crude language. The sun was lowering itself in the western sky and there was a slight chill in the air and Carl was hungry. When we got to the street we went to the East River's edge and looked out longingly at our home borough of Queens on the other side of the river. Low rolling white cap waves moved in the river as we inhaled the faint moist air.

As I looked south, the Williamsburg Bridge looked so far away that my chest felt heavy and while I wasn't hungry my stomach was queasy. Then Jack who was looking north said, "You know the Triborough Bridge looks closer."

Carl and I turned our heads north. Then Carl said, "Yeah, but where the hell does that bring you down in Queens?"

"Who cares," Jack said, "we'll figure that out when we get back to Queens." Jack broke away from the rail and started walking north along the river-walk.

"Let's go,' I said to Carl as we began to follow Jack. "How far is it – do you know?"

"No, I know it's in the hundreds though." Carl answered, "maybe a hundred-twenty something street?" We caught up to Jack and continued on together as the sun continued to move lower in the sky and long shadows were cast our way from tall buildings to our left. After almost a mile and a half we reached Gracie Mansion at Eighty-ninth Street. We took a minute or two to marvel at being this close to the Mayor's residence. But another disappointment was about to confront us. As we continued on up just a bit further we saw the deep hooked bend in the coast line that we would have to walk if we continued to the Triborough Bridge. The irregular uptown Manhattan coastline had played a cruel trick on us making the Triborough Bridge look closer than it actually was. We all looked at each other as if we could read each other's thoughts. And the big question was – What to do, now?

Then Carl blurted out, "I'm hungry, I'm starving, I haven't had anything to eat all day."

"I got fifteen cents," I said as I pulled a nickel and a dime out of my pocket, "You got anything, Jack?"

"Nope."

"Carl?" I asked.

"No, nothing – because I had no idea where I was going today."

Jack let out a long breath and said. "Ok, what do we do now? It's starting to get dark now...."

"We got to call somebody – somebody at home," I said.

"I ain't call'in home – my dad will kill me." Jack said

I looked at Carl but he nodded his head side to side, "Not me either."

"Ok, I'll call... let's go find a phone booth." I said.

We reversed course and then cut right along Eighty-second Street towards Second Avenue. After a few blocks as we approached a fruit stand Carl begged me to spend my nickel to buy an apple that he just had to have. Carl got his apple and I kept fingering the dime in my pocket to make sure it was there as we walked on. In a few more blocks we finally came to a drug store that had a phone booth and I made the fateful call to my house. Jack and Carl held the phone booth door open and chimed in as I tried to explain to my dad as best as I could what had happened today. Dad asked a million rapid-fire questions in between my story but it ended with one question and one directive. "Are you sure you're all ok?" and "Get yourselves back down to the foot of the Fifty-ninth Street Bridge and I'll pick you all up with the car – as soon as I call Jack and Carl's parents. Just be careful and get yourselves down there!"

The sun was falling behind the horizon as the weary Musketeers (Athos, Porthos, and Aramis) walked down Second Avenue and continued through the seventies and the sixties until we finally landed at the Fifty-ninth Street Bridge Plaza. Our timing was perfect – in just a few anxious silent moments we saw my dad's old gray Chevy coming off the bridge. Dad waved his hand signaling to us to get in position near the traffic light so he could stop to pick us up – d'Artagnan had arrived to the rescue!

In the next few minutes my dad circled the block, picked us up and we were on our way across the bridge. I won't go into what happened when we got home but I will say that our great story was told all around the neighborhood – it was the stuff that legends are made of like Davey Crockett wrestling with a bear. And we did stand at the top of our block and point out at the Empire State Building and told people about how we walked there.

. . .

Well that's about it – that's all there is to tell about the big adventure. We never had another adventure like that again. Except for the time that Jack lost me on the subway when we were coming home from the Museum of Natural History and I met a lady in a bakery who drove me in her car to Queens Boulevard and I had to walk home past the cemetery at night – but that's another story.

> **Author's Note**
> This story may seem like fiction but only the dialogue was embellished. Jack DeRidder, Carl Abbe and I really did this in our youthful days of boyhood exploration.

about the authors

Katrenia Grace Busch is a freelance journalist whose work has appeared in NPR, CBS, as well as local newspapers. Her award-winning poem titled, "*Mystery and Wind*" took 2nd place in the 2022 League for Innovative Creative Writing contest. She continues to serve as a poetry editor for The Bookends Review and is on the editorial board for the American Psychological Association's Psychology of Consciousness: Theory, Research and Practice. She is a federal grant reviewer for the U.S. Department of Justice. Her work can be found in *Red Penguin Books, Bloom Magazine, The Trouvaille Review, October Hill, Literature Today* amongst others. She can be found on Facebook here: https://www.facebook.com/share/15fooLK5EE/?mibextid=wwXIfr

---

Paul DiSclafani is a retired Health Care IT Professional and an award-winning columnist. His column, Long Island Living, has garnered numerous awards from the Press Club of Long Island (PCLI). The PCLI recognized Long Island Living as the Best Column in 2021, and in 2025, his story, "The other 'R' Word," placed first in the Narrative-Humor category. Overall, his column and individual stories have amassed 10 awards since 2018.

He has published three memoirs with Red Penguin Publishing: *Burning Through the West Coast* (2020), *Long Island Living* (2022), and *Meeting Bruce Springsteen* (2024).

Paul and his wife Barbara relocated to Ocala, Florida, in 2025 after 68 years of life in Brooklyn and Long Island. His son James resides in Massapequa, NY, while Kevin and his wife Arielle live in North Carolina. You can read his columns, view video appearances, purchase books, and keep in touch at www.pauldisclafani.com

---

The author of six books, **Mark Fleisher** has won awards from the Military Writers Society of America and SouthWest Writers. He holds a journalism degree from Ohio University and worked as a reporter and editor in New York and Washington, D.C.. His Air Force service included a year in Vietnam as a combat news reporter, earning a Bronze Star. He and his wife, Merle Pokempner, a retired art therapist, live in Albuquerque's North Valley. They have no cats, dogs or other distractions.

Jordan Frazier is a poet and writer who is passionate about storytelling and nature. A life-long resident of Pennsylvania and a graduate of East Stroudsburg University with a B.A in English, he began honing his craft at the age of 19 and he's been writing ever since. Jordan enjoys music, nature walks and archeology. His next adventure will find him exploring both the urban and bucolic landscapes of central Virginia and bringing those experiences to life through his poetry.

Dennis Hawkins is 79-year-old man who has been "around the block" in NYC since he was 2 years old. Having lived during a time when a plethora of tabloids called out to him on city newsstands, he learned to write poetry by absorbing headlines which fit Ezra Pound's definition of poetry as language "charged with meaning." After retiring a couple of years ago from his many years as a prosecutor and anti-corruption advisor, he revisited his first love – writing poetry. His poetry has been published in the NY Times – *City Room*, *The Poetry Distillery*, *Password* (a journal of very short poetry), and included as the closing entry of the novel, *Fallen Angel III*, by Michael Vecchione.

Suzanne Kamata is an American permanent resident of Japan. She is the author several books including the travel memoirs *A Girls' Guide to the Islands* (Gemma Open Door, 2017) and *Squeaky Wheels: Travels with my Daughter by Train, Plane, Metro, Tuk-tuk and Wheelchair* (Wyatt-Mackenzie Publishing, 2019), and the short fiction collection *River of Dolls and Other Stories* (Penguin Random House SEA, 2025). Her most recent novel, *Cinnamon Beach* (Wyatt-Mackenzie Publishing, 2024) was named Best Beach Read in the 2024 Zibby Awards and won the Los Angeles Book Festival prize for General Fiction. She earned an MFA from the University of British Columbia and is currently an associate professor at Naruto University of Education, where she enjoys introducing her students to the work of Dorothy Parker and Langston Hughes. She lives in Tokushima Prefecture with her husband and two cats, Mii and Sumi.

Michael P. Kusen is an author, illustrator and retired chess educator who has created seven instructional chess books and several poetry chapbooks – some of which are in the Poets House Library Collection in Manhattan. He also has published a family history and his essays, short stories and poems have appeared in several anthologies. His poems and cover art have appeared in <u>The Performance Poets Annual Anthologies</u>. Michael continues to create poetry and essay chapbooks while juggling several background projects including illustrated poems, video poems and assemblage art. mqsen@aol.com

Mark Lord was born in Brooklyn and raised in Puerto Rico, where his lifelong devotion to the theater began. He is a retired New York City public school teacher, a freelance journalist and an enthusiastic participant in community theater—as an actor, director and playwright.

Several of his plays have been produced, including *Let's Hear It For Queens,* a musical tribute to the borough he now calls home, an excerpt of which was published in the anthology, *Act One: One Act Vol. 2* in 2018. His book *The Theater and I* is a peek into community and professional theater in New York, joined by his Facebook community.

Antoinette Truglio Martin is a teacher and award winning children's book author who loves to share her bookish events with kids of all ages. She is a retired speech therapist and special ed teacher, who now enjoys life as a children's book author, memoirist, and blogger. She wrote the memoir, *Hug Everyone You Know: A Year of Community, Courage, and Cancer* (She Writes Press), the award winning middle-grade historical fiction series, *Becoming America's Stories* (Red Penguin Books), and the picture book, *Famous Seaweed Soup* (Purple Butterfly Press). Be sure to visit her website and blog, Stories Served Around The Table at StoriesServed.com.

Lisa Diaz Meyer is the dark fiction author and poet of award-winning books, *All Roads Home, All Roads Destined,* and *All Roads Shattered.* Her work can also be found in several anthologies published by Red Penguin Books, the Bards Annual, Local Gems Press, and Nassau County Voices In Verse. Born and raised in Brooklyn, New York, she now hails from southern Long Island with her family and rescue cat, Chloe.

William John Rostron's books have been read on four continents and all fifty states. His *Band in the Wind* series of novels (steeped in the 1960s music and culture), has received critical acclaim from Writers Digest, the Online Book Club Review, and have all received Amazon ratings of 4.5 out of 5, or higher. He has published over four dozen short stories in anthologies, with five receiving awards from Writers Digest. All of these pieces also appear in *his* short story compilations, *A Flamingo Under the Carousel* and *T-Rex Stole My Computer*. Five of his stories have been produced on the New York stage (available for viewing on the author's website) He recently edited the Red Penguin anthology, KAPOW. www.WilliamJohnRostron.com

---

Laura Shenton is probably best known for her music non-fiction, particularly Dance With The Devil – The Cozy Powell Story (Wymer Publishing) and Tommy Bolin – In and Out of Deep Purple (Sonicbond Publishing).

Her fiction books are character-driven with a short, punchy narrative that gets straight to the point – typically novellas and novelettes. Genres include gothic, fantasy, and adventure (mostly, with the occasional diversion).

Laura's children's books are simple, accessible, and fun – an excellent choice for youngsters with fertile imaginations who are just beginning their reading journey.

Jim Tritten is a retired Navy carrier pilot who lives in Corrales, New Mexico, with his Danish author/artist wife and an ever-changing number of cats. He is the recipient of eighty-four national and regional writing awards, which include the Alfred Thayer Mahan Award from the Navy League of the United States for literary achievement in 1986, the 2023 Writer of the Year from the Military Writers Society of America, and the 2023 recipient of the Parris Award from SouthWest Writers.

Janet Metz Walter's first book for Red Penguin was an anthology of real stories called *The 2 Carrot Ring and Other Fascinating Jewelry Stories*. She does interactive programs with organizations where participants tell their own personal jewelry stories. She is also a mentor to beginning authors, and a book reviewer, as well as a teacher of the game of Mah Jongg among the several other positions she has held.

As a former travel agent she was thrilled to be able to travel the world and all 50 states with her husband and two children, partially using her "Unexpected Gift." There were special things about every place she traveled to but at the moment her favorite city in Europe is Barcelona because of all the fabulous architecture by Antoni Gaudi.

She has contributed stories to seven anthologies including *London*, *Rome*, and *New York*, and hopes to be able to share some more of her million stories of her experiences.

Lynn Zimmering found herself at the beginning of COVID-19 living alone in her one-bedroom apartment on Manhattan's East Side with nothing to do.

After about six weeks, she was so bored that she was ready to scream. Instead of screaming, she wrote her feelings as a blog, and she felt calmer. So, she wrote another blog and felt even more satisfied. By last count, she has written 225 blogs, published in two books: "My Pandemic Paradox," volumes 1 and 2. Writing is her latest career, the ninth one.

There were no more acting classes, flute lessons (or the need to practice), no more volunteer work with dementia residents at the Jewish Home in Rochleigh, NJ, and no more meetings with friends when it was warm enough to eat outside. Writing was the perfect career for living alone with nothing to do. Writing filled her days.

In the past, she had her own business as a recruiter, then worked for Unilever as a Supervisor in the call center, and then worked for Weight Watchers as a meeting leader. She also worked for Bloomindale's on their Executive Training Squad to prepare for a career in retailing. And then, she became a Life Coach, and for a short time, she was a photographer.

Who knows what she might do next?

also from travel tales & tips

London: Smokes, Blokes, and Jokes of Foggy Town
Paris: Love, Loss and Longing in the City of Lights
Rome: Centuries of Stories of the Eternal City

www.ingramcontent.com/pod-product-compliance
Lightning Source LLC
Chambersburg PA
CBHW052144070526
44585CB00017B/1961